STUDIES IN LEVITICAL TERMINOLOGY, I

The Encroacher and the Levite
The Term 'Aboda

STUDIES IN
LEVITICAL TERMINOLOGY, I

The Encroacher and the Levite
The Term 'Aboda

By JACOB MILGROM

WIPF & STOCK · Eugene, Oregon

Wipf and Stock Publishers
199 W 8th Ave, Suite 3
Eugene, OR 97401

Studies in Levitcal Terminology
The Encroacher and the Levite the Term 'Aboda
By Milgrom, Jacob
Copyright©1970 by Milgrom, Jacob
ISBN 13: 978-1-4982-9288-7
Publication date 3/8/2016
Previously published by University of California Press, 1970

CONTENTS

I. Introduction
  § a. The purpose 1
  § b. The methodology 1
  § c. Acknowledgments 4

II. The Encroacher and the Levite: הזר הקרב יומת

זר and יומת 5
  § 1. זר 5
  § 2. יומת 5
  § 3. Deductions 8

שמר משמרת 8
  § 4. Definition 8
  § 5. The Levites in P 9
  § 6. "For the Lord" 10
  § 7. משמרת in Chronicles . . . 12
  § 8. Recapitulation 15

קרב 16
  § 9. The hypothesis 16
  § 10. Numbers 1:51 17
  § 11. Numbers 3:10 17
  § 12. Numbers 3:38 17
  § 13. Numbers 18:7 18
  § 14. Korah 18
  § 15. The clarification of קרב . . 19
  § 16. The principle of intention . . . 20
  § 17. Why יומת 21
  § 18. The wrong principle 21
  § 19. Why ימות 22

והם ישאו עונם 22
  § 20. The problem 22
  § 21. Solution 1 25
  § 22. Resolving the subject . . . 25

§ 23. Resolving the pericope   26
§ 24. Resolving the formula   27
§ 25. Resolving the object   27
§ 26. Two more solutions   27
§ 27. A new verse   28
§ 28. The Levites' *kippur*   28
§ 29. Recapitulation   31
§ 30. The new principle   32

Permissive קרב/נגש   33
§ 31. Definition   33
§ 32. Distribution   33
§ 33. נגש   34
§ 34. Nuzi and the ancient Near East   35
§ 35. Nuzi *qrb*   36
§ 36. Conclusions   36

The Disqualified Priest   38
§ 37. The cases   38
§ 38. The sanctuary   39
§ 39. The altar   41
§ 40. The distinctions   42
§ 41. Recapitulation   43

The Sinaitic Precedent   44
§ 42. Nachmanides   44
§ 43. Other parallels   44

Origins   46
§ 44. Clues   46
§ 45. Levi the Tribe   48
§ 46. The Priests and Phineas   48
§ 47. The final clue: shared custody   49
§ 48. The Hittite "Instruction for Temple Officials"   50
§ 49. Recapitulation   53
§ 50. The antiquity of the formula   54
§ 51. The contrasts   56

III. The Term עבדה

The Levitical עבדה   60
§ 52. The error   60
§ 53. Definitions   60
§ 54. General removal   61
§ 55. The components   61

§ 56. Numbers, chapter 4 62
§ 57. Clan distinctions 62
§ 58. The censuses 64
§ 59. Recapitulation 65
§ 60. Numbers 4:19*b* and the LXX 65
§ 61. Post-conquest עבדה 66
§ 62. Samuel 68
§ 63. Chronicles 71
§ 64. Composite of Levitic עבדה 72

עבדה in P 76
§ 65. The Pentateuch 76
§ 66. מלאכה 77
§ 67. Its three meanings 77
§ 68. מלאכה in Exodus 36:1–7 79
§ 69. Festivals 80
§ 70. Census silver 81
§ 71. The paradox 82

עבדה in Later Biblical Sources 82
§ 72. Chronicles 82
§ 73. Ezekiel's midrash on P 83
§ 74. Nehemiah's midrash on עבדה 86
§ 75. Recapitulation and conclusion 87

Indices
Bibliography 91
Abbreviations Not Explained in Text 95
Terms Discussed 97
References 99

I. INTRODUCTION

§ a. *The Purpose*. This monograph is a study of the formula הזר הקרב יומת
and its related terminology. It represents the first in a projected series of studies
on the laws of the contamination and desecration of sancta as found in the
Priestly source of the Bible (abbreviated P). The job profile of the priesthood
drawn up by P itself, and repeated by the prophet-priest Ezekiel, calls for
teaching the distinctions "between the holy (קדש) and the common (חל), and
between the impure (טמא) and the pure (טהור)."[1] These four categories can
interact by pairs in six different ways. Theoretically there are even more interactions since the realm of the holy comprises two distinct subcategories, "the
most sacred" (קדש קדשים) and "the sacred" (קדש). However, since the common
and the holy are presumed to be pure—their normal and acceptable condition—
it follows that, in reality, a total of five interactions take place, as follows:
(1) the most sacred and the common, (2) the most sacred and the impure, (3) the
sacred and the common, (4) the sacred and the impure, and (5) the common and
the impure.

This monograph discusses the first of these interacting pairs, but does not
exhaust it. For example, omitted from consideration, is another cultic formula
כל הנגע יקדש which also falls under the purview of most sacred–common contacts. Thus, this initial offering is but a small fraction of the projected enterprise,
and it should be seen in that light. In fact, the very definition of the four categories—what precisely is meant by the holy, the common, the impure, the pure
and how they are marked off from each other—must await a later stage. For
only after a sufficient number of correlations have been accumulated and
analyzed can any inductive generalizations rightfully take place.

§ b. *The Methodology*. My investigation is confined to the P source, but it
will make no assumptions regarding its substrata. Modern critics, however,
insist on the reverse procedure. For example: "It is furthermore not possible to
confront the book of Ezekiel as a unity and the Zadokite program as part of
this unity either with P or with an ostensibly earlier but in reality later stratum
of P (for example, Num. 16f.) and, then, to pose the question of priority. This is
definitely passé. One can only attempt to compare specific strata of P with

---

[1] Lev. 10:10; see Ezek. 22:26, 44:23; also Lev. 14:57, 15:31.

I

specific strata of Ezekiel."[2] I submit this statement is correct theoretically but incorrect methodologically. For there is nothing more fluid and moot in modern biblical scholarship than the exact bounds of the substrata of any given literary unit. To take P, as a case in point, there is no concensus concerning its composition: e.g., von Rad presumes two continuous strata,[3] but Elliger dissects portions of P into as many as nine (excluding glosses and secondary additions!).[4] To be sure, P is a literary composite; the symbiosis of mutually contradictory laws can point to no other conclusion: e.g., the tithes (Lev. 27:30 and Num. 18:21) and the communal *ḥaṭṭ'āṭ* sacrifice (Lev. 4:13–21 and Num. 15:24–26). However, to derive consequences for the history of the Bible and its institutions on the basis of unproven "specific strata" would be to erect imposing structures on quicksand.

The advantage of this procedure will become manifest in the study itself. In the case of two terms, my conclusions will logically lead to the question of historical background, which I shall be free to explore precisely because there will be no straitjacketing by a priori assumptions concerning the exact stratification within P. Specifically, P's concept of the Tabernacle, משמרת (in light of the formula הזר הקרב יומת) will be measured against the historical attestation of this function in Israel and the ancient Near East. In the other instance, I will show that עבדה in P is totally different from its meaning in similar contexts in the later literature. In both cases, I will arrive at new conclusions concerning their origins.[5] The reader, however, is not to expect the formulation of a new set of criteria for dating biblical material. This is a study of cultic terms and, at best, I can but allude to their literary, historical, and comparative religious implications. Perhaps these leads will be regarded as intrinsically meritorious and so induce other scholars to follow up their pursuit.

An investigation of the cultic terminology of ancient Israel confronts two main difficulties. First, the cult is a hoary institution whose peculiar vocabulary and meaning was often unknown to the age of the second Temple, not to speak of subsequent generations. Second, the evidence at hand is so sparse that at times it allows only a darkened glimpse of the underlying usage but is insufficient to define it.

---

[2] A. H. J. Gunneweg, *Leviten und Priester, FRLANT* (1965) 197.

[3] G. von Rad, *Die Priesterschrift im Hexateuch, BWANT* 65 (1934).

[4] K. Elliger, *Leviticus, HAT* (1966).

[5] Two caveats concerning the use of terminology as a chronological criterion should be sounded at once: (a) We may not be dealing with strictly technical terms, in which case a word may have multiple nuances; see the sage warning of W. G. Lambert "Literary Style in First Millenium Mesopotamia" *JAOS* (1968) 88:124, n. 2. (b) Even technical terms occasionally exhibit a protean character, e.g., מלאכה (§§ 66–69), קדש (n. 149), מקדש (n. 78); the fluidity, however, is within the narrow range of derived meaning. Nonetheless, whenever two bodies of literature use the same terms—indeed, even the same texts—in totally different and mutually exclusive ways, chronological distinctions can be suspected, e.g., עבדה (§§ 52–75) and partially, משמרת (§§ 4–8).

The text itself offers the greatest help; it has been excellently preserved, and the few variants found in the Versions are nearly always inferior to the Masoretic text. Equally significant is that both above-mentioned difficulties can be attacked from positions outside the Bible. The institutions of ancient Israel are being progressively elucidated by the unearthed cultic and legal texts of the second millennium Near East. In our present study, we shall have the opportunity, more than once, of illuminating obscure technical terms (and the role of the Levites) by resort to these texts. However, a caveat must be sounded. Not all parallel customs are due to borrowing and more importantly, they may be interpreted within each culture in different and even contradictory ways.

Israel's technical cultic vocabulary also finds elucidation in another literature —one largely neglected: that of post-biblical Judaism. Its earliest statements are contemporaneous with the end of the second Temple, and since the cult is a conservative institution—being extremely resistant to change—many of the practices and terms preserved in rabbinical literature may hark back to biblical times. Here too a demurrer must be entered. The antiquity of a ritual does not imply that it always carried the same meaning. To the contrary, as seen in the history of all religions, the same cultic act can constantly undergo reinterpretation in response to the spiritual needs of succeeding generations. In Judaism, moreover, as disagreements among the Rabbis demonstrate, both rite and reason have often been forgotten. Nonetheless, with these precautions in mind, the extra-biblical literature—of Israel's contemporary and anterior environment and of its own creative continuum—rings with many suggestive echoes for the listening ear.

It is thus inevitable that this monograph, and subsequent ones which may emerge, be a study in cult terminology, focusing in this initial stage upon the problem of encroachment upon sancta as illustrated by the injunction הזר הקרב יומת. Each term of the formula will be scanned for its meaning within P and without, and wherever other technical terms cluster in the shadow of this formula, the same procedure will be applied to them. Since the term עבדה exhibits extraordinary distribution and implications, it has been reserved for independent discussion. Altogether, sixty scriptural terms are analyzed. In some instances they lead to new conclusions which, if correct, mandate both a retranslation of whole chapters of the Bible and a reconsideration of Israel's religious life and thought.

Here an apology is in order. Since only a few major terms are taken up in my text (e.g., עבדה, משמרת, קרב) typographical propriety should have relegated the remaining terms to the end of the study in the form of appendices. However, the terms in question number some fifty odd; moreover, they are inextricably tied to the major terms and must be discussed with them. This would force the reader into perpetual motion, flipping incessantly from the text to the appendices. For this reason, I have treated the minor terms as footnotes. This has led to a bulky apparatus, but it gives the reader the convenience of studying a related term on the very page where it is mentioned in the text.

One last procedural item. I have omitted the customary preface on the present status of research on the terms selected for study, which would have entailed a long bibliographical list for each rejected meaning. Instead, I have chosen to cite the meanings accepted by the standard lexicons, and I shall cite them seriatim, as they occur in the discussion. I have singled out individual critics only whenever they have proposed other interpretations and especially when they have anticipated my own. Thus, if my own work will not be seen in its proper light with respect to previous research in the introduction, it will be so seen in the study, not at once, but cumulatively.

§ c. *Acknowledgments.* I could not conclude without recognizing those whose help was indispensable to my work. I am particularly grateful that I can count among my closest confidants, my teacher, Professor H. L. Ginsberg, and my friend, Professor Moshe Greenberg, both of whom, in my eyes, stand *primi inter pares* among the scholars of their respective generations. My debt to them goes far beyond their critical comments on the drafts of this study and of previous opera, for their inspiration and encouragement have, indeed, motivated my career.

Experts in many fields graciously aided me in oral and written communications—in addition to their published works—and my acknowledgments to them are gratefully recorded in the footnotes. I must single out a special group of them—my colleagues on the faculty of the Department of Near Eastern Languages of the University of California, Berkeley, whose mastery of allied disciplines was at my beck and call. Especially do I wish to name Professors Anne Kilmer and Leonard Lesko for their respective assyriological and egyptological assistance and Professor Joshua Blau, on sabbatical from the Hebrew University, for being a willing and effective sounding board for many of my ideas. A word on the Berkeley collegium would not be complete without special thanks to its chairman, Professor William Brinner, for fostering an atmosphere of harmony and confidence essential to creative labor. Also to be thanked are Professors D. N. Freedman, J. Muilenburg, W. Zimmerli, and Père R. de Vaux o.p. for their valuable criticisms of my first draft.

Finally to Jo and our children I offer my gratitude for their strength, faith, and, above all, for cheerfully relinquishing the time rightfully belonging to them. May they and all who invested their energy and knowledge in me find in this monograph a small but worthy return.

Jacob Milgrom

II. THE ENCROACHER AND THE LEVITE:

הזר הקרב יומת

זר AND יומת

The formula הזר הקרב יומת occurs four times, all in the book of Numbers (1:51; 3:10, 38; 18:7); each word merits separate investigation.

§ 1. זר. The use of זר in P is specific and unambiguous. It always refers to a person who is unauthorized to perform the cultic act in question; usually he is a non-priest,[6] and his crime is punishable by death. Who is his executioner, God or man? This problem is more complex, for it hinges on the meaning of יומת.

§ 2. יומת. The agent of יומת is never given or explained. Rabbinic exegesis of this formula is that death is at the hands of God,[7] as is always the case whenever

---

[6] E.g., Exod. 29:33, 30:33; Lev. 22:10–12. However, the זר may also be a "non-Levite": e.g., Num. 1:51, which explicitly refers to encroachment upon the Levites, see § 10 and Num. 18:4, where the זר who may not associate (יקרב) with the priest excludes the Levite (so v. 2a, הקרב אתך). M. Haran identifies the זר exclusively with the non-priest (see his pioneering and definitive work, "The Priestly Image of the Tabernacle," *HUCA* [1965] 191–226, esp. 222), and for evidence, he cites: "that no זר, one not of Aaron's offspring, should presume to offer incense" (Num. 17:5 [16:40 KJV]). This text, however, presents the contrary impression. It explicitly mentions the offering of incense, a function reserved exclusively to the priesthood. Moreover, if זר dogmatically applies to the non-priest, then the phrase "one of Aaron's offspring" is superfluous. The latter must, therefore, qualify the prior, more general term זר and tells us that not only the זר but even the non-Aaronide (including the Levite) must not offer incense. It can therefore be argued that this verse teaches that the Levite is not a זר. In any case, it must be ruled out as evidence for Haran.

Swinging to the opposite pole is L. A. Snijders' "The meaning of *zar*," *OTS* (1954) 10:1–154, esp. 124ff. (the only other study, to my knowledge, to investigate this formula, but which is to be used with caution, see infra nn. 62, 141). He argues that the formula refers to the Israelite in all four instances. I shall demonstrate that neither extreme is correct but that Num. 1:51, 3:38 have in mind the Israelite and 3:10, 18:7 the Levite. Snijders further defines the זר as "the layman who has withdrawn from Y," on which see infra n. 83.

[7] M Sanh 9:6, Sifre Zuta (on Num. 18:7), and Y Sanh 48b (acc. to the correction of the Pnei Moshe); however, a strong minority opinion is registered for death by man, see R. Akiba, R. Yochanan b Nuri, ad. loc. (and R. Yishmael acc. to Sifre, Num. 116, but B Sanh 83a reverses his position). The Targums also clearly read "put to death," followed by Ibn Ezra (on Num. 1:51).

capital punishment is decreed for purely cultic violations. However, a careful examination of all יומת loci in P reveals that, without exception, death by man is meant. Indeed the *hofʻal*, יומת, can only mean "be put to death," i.e., by man. This textual and grammatical observation will be brought into sharper focus by observing how P distinguishes between ימות (*qal*) and יומת (*hofʻal*), paying particular attention to those religious crimes where either term might be used. For convenience the verses in question are tabulated according to subject matter; proof that the *qal* and *hofʻal* ascribe the execution of death to God and man, respectively,[8] is brought in the notes for each case separately.

TABLE A

יומת (rather than ימות, *qal*) in P

Violation	Source
1. Sabbath[9]	Exod. 31:14f., 35:2; Num. 15:35
2. Illicit sex[10]	Lev. 19:20, 20:10, 11, 12, 13, 15, 16
3. Molech[11]	Lev. 20:2
4. Blasphemy[12]	Lev. 24:16
5. Abusing parents[13]	Lev. 20:9
6. Proscribed person[14]	Lev. 27:29
7. Playing the medium[15]	Lev. 20:27
8. Ascending Mount Sinai[16]	Exod. 19:12

[8] P also uses כרת to indicate death by divine agency, but the study of this term must, perforce, await my discussion of biblical impurities. In the interim see W. Zimmerli, "Die Eigenart der prophetische Rede des Ezechiel," *ZAW* (1954) 66:1–26, esp. 13–19; M. Tsevat, "Studies in the Book of Samuel," I, *HUCA* (1961) 32:191–216; and infra nn. 9–11, 20.

[9] Death is by stoning (Num. 15:35). As to the meaning of כרת and יומת in the same passage, see the similar situation for the Molech worshipper (Lev. 20-1-5) and our solution infra in nn. 10, 214.

[10] Death by man in these verses is confirmed by (a) the historical narratives, e.g., Dinah (Gen. 34:31); the concubine at Gibeah (Judg. 20:13); (b) the synonyms דמיו בו/דמיהם בם (vv. 11, 12, 13, 16; cf. Exod. 22:1; Deut. 19:10; Judg. 9:24; 1 Kings 2:33, 37—clear cases of bloodguilt for homicide) and the explicit mention of death by burning (v. 14); and (c) the literary structure of the chapter which divides itself up into an ordered series of graduated penalties, as follows: vv. 9–16 מות, vv. 17–19 כרת, vv. 20–21 עריריrim (childless). The clear distinction between מות and כרת clauses and the diminishing severity in the arrangement prove that the initial penalties (מות) must refer to immediate death by man.

An objection may be raised that in a parallel listing of these sex crimes (Lev. 18) the penalty of כרת is imposed for all of them (v. 29). My answer is the same as for the simultaneous occurrence of יומת and כרת in the Molech and Sabbath violations, that God promises to intervene (כרת) against the said offenders in the contingency that the community does not put them to death (יומת). See also the similar conclusions of M. Greenberg, "Crimes and Punishments," *IDB*, I (1962) A.2(end), and S. E. Loewenstamm, "*Kārēt*," *Ency. Miq.* IV (1962) cols. 330–332 (Heb.).

[11] Death is by stoning (v. 2b). For the double penalty of כרת and יומת, see supra n. 10 on sexual crimes and infra n. 214.

TABLE B

מות, *qal* (rather than *hof'al*, הומת/יומת) in P

Violator	Violation	Source
1. High Priest	Improper entry to shrine[17]	Lev. 16:2, 13
2. Priest	Improper officiation[18]	Exod. 28:43, 30:20f.; Lev. 10:9
3. Priest	Prohibited mourning[19]	Lev. 10:6
4. Priest	Delinquent "guarding"[20]	Lev. 22:9
5. Levites	Touching covered sancta[21]	Num. 4:15
6. Levites	Viewing interior sancta (uncovered)[22]	Num. 4:19f.
7. Levites	קרב[23]	Num. 18:3
8. Laymen	קרב[24]	Num. 17:28, 18:22

[12] Death is by stoning (v. 23; see 1 Kings 21:10, 13f.). See also infra n. 214.

[13] See supra n. 5 on the literary structure and vocabulary of Lev. 20. Also cf. its parallel in the Covenant Code (Exod. 21:17)—in the context of civil statutes.

[14] See Deut. 13:16 "by the sword"; Judg. 21:10f.; 1 Sam. 15:3*b*, 18; 1 Kings 20:42; Mesha, 17.

[15] The manner of death is illustrated by King Saul (1 Sam. 28:9).

[16] Explicitly defined by following verse: "he shall either be stoned or pierced" (v. 13). See § 43 on the relevance of this pericope, though outside of P.

[17] Since 16:1f. is the redactoral link between 10:3ff. and ch. 10, the threatened death of the high priest is in the manner of Nadab and Abihu, i.e., by God.

[18] The same penalty is invoked for the priest who officiates while improperly washed (Exod. 30:20), improperly dressed (Exod. 28:43), physically unfit (Lev. 21:23), or intoxicated (Lev. 10:9). The high priest has additional criteria for proper dress (Exod. 28:35). For the distinctions between the sanctuary and the altar in regard to these violations, see "The Disqualified Priest," §§ 37–41.

[19] This rule is restricted to the seven-day consecration period (contrast Lev. 21:2; Ezek. 44:25). The high priest is permanently enjoined from observing mourning rites (Lev. 21:10) but no penalties are listed.

[20] Lev. 22:9 concludes the first unit of this chapter (vv. 3–9) and undoubtedly refers to the danger for a contaminated priest in coming into contact with sacred food, see n. 152 infra. The penalty for impurity-holiness contact, it will be separately shown, is clearly established as כרת. Therefore the death decree here (ומתו בו) must be at the hands of God. Also, for the meaning of משמרת, "guarding" in this passage, see § 6.

[21] The most sacred objects are covered so that the Kohathites may carry them when the Wilderness camp is in transit. However, their porterage is by means of staves, for these sancta can transmit a fatal charge even through their covers. For amplification, see § 57. That death is through divine agency, see 1 Sam. 6:19.

[22] This prohibition does not apply to the outer altar, even though it is a "most sacred" object, see § 40 on "Disqualified Priest." What applies to Levites is, of course, also true for laymen (see Neh. 6:11).

[23] See infra n. 76.

[24] The full meaning of this violation is the burden of this chapter; see §§ 11–19. Its exposition will reveal that it is no exception at all. For the immediate purpose, note that this למות is in the same context with קצף/נגף. Since the latter issues solely from God, death by divine agency must be meant. See further § 19.

§ 3. *Deductions.* Tables A and B clearly demonstrate that (1) P is most scrupulous in the use of the *qal* and *hofʿal* of מות whenever it wishes to distinguish respectively between death by God or man:[25] יומת of the formula must, therefore, mean death by man; and (2) crimes against the sanctuary are all in table B, i.e., death is by God.[26] These observations are bewildering, for they only throw into clearer relief the anomalous character of the formula. How, indeed, can we explain that it alone demands that a capital crime against the sanctuary be punished by man and not by God?

To answer this question is the main burden of this chapter, but my assault on this problem must necessarily be postponed until I have cleared all the obstacles along the way. The terms of the formula must be defined and their implications fully explored. Let us return to the term יומת. Having established that the death sentence is executed by man, we are left to ask: Which man? Can we identify the executioner? The answer is contingent upon a precise understanding of the idiom שמר משמרת which proliferates in the contexts of the formula (Num. 1:53, 3:7–10, 3:38, 18:3–7), and to which I now turn.

שמר משמרת

§ 4. *Definition.* משמרת in connection with the Tabernacle/Tent of Meeting means "guard duty," *and nothing else.*[27] This usage is not the invention of P but

---

[25] Ezekiel, strongly influenced by P, scrupulously uses the *qal* when he means death by God (see esp. 3:17ff., 18:4 et passim, 33:7ff. and M. Greenberg, "Some Postulates of Biblical Criminal Law," *Y. Kaufmann Jubilee* Vol. [1960] 21f.) On this basis, it has been conjectured that יומת of Ezek. 18:13 is an error for ימות. (So many versions, see BH⁴. and cf. 3:18, 20, 33:6, 8.) However דמיו בו יהיה which follows מות יומת (ibid.) is attested only in cases where judicial execution is intended. (Contrast Lev. 9–16 with vv. 17–21 and see W. Zimmerli, *Ezechiel* BK, 1959 13:6, 410f.). Moreover as K. Koch has shown, "Der Spruch 'Sein Blut bleibe auf seinem Haupt'" *VT* (1962) 12:396–416, this idiom implies that the bloodguilt will rest not upon him but upon his *human* executioner. The emendation is therefore, unwarranted.

[26] Another important deduction is that death by God, expressed by the *qal* מות, is meted out to priests and Levites but never to laymen; see infra n. 76 for the discussion. As for the ostensible exception of B8, supra, there is no difficulty for the verses in question (Num. 17:28, 18:22) frame a pericope whose main teaching is that the situation whereby laymen have died at the hands of God (for the sin of קרב) will take place no more. See §§ 17f., 24, and 30.

[27] This is the brilliant observation of Abarbanel (on Num. 3:5) though I cannot subscribe to all his interpretations, see infra n. 30. Ibn Ezra anticipates him in a single verse (on Num. 3:8) but does not follow up his insight (he abandons it in the previous comment!). To my knowledge, Abarbanel's viewpoint was abandoned by all his successors and was resurrected in our day by Haran, "Priestly Image," pp. 221–223, who it seems has arrived at his conclusion independently. It is of interest that Rashi (on Num. 3:1) who defines משמרת as "any post to which a person is appointed and (the duties) which he is bound to carry out"—the view followed by all lexicons and translations (see infra n. 51)—is constrained to resort to a Talmudic example (Meg 13b) to prove his case.

is found in all the sources. Indeed, the primary and probably original meaning of משמרת is "watch post" (e.g., Isa. 21:8; Hab. 2:1)[28] and of the full idiom שמר משמרת is "do guard duty for," e.g., the palace (2 Kings 11:5; 1 Chron. 12:29).[29]

§ 5. *The Levites in P.* שמר משמרת in P is especially associated with the function of the Levites, the locus classicus for which is: "The Levites, however, shall encamp around the Tabernacle of the Pact that wrath may not strike the Israelite community; the Levites shall do guard duty for the Tabernacle of the Pact" (Num. 1:53). Thus the Levitic encampment is blueprinted from the outset as a protective cordon around the sacred area.

Moreover, guard duty is a lifelong responsibility. The hard labor of dismantling, transporting, and reassembling the Tabernacle (called עבדה)[30] ceases at age fifty, but משמרת continues on (Num. 8:24–26). Two entire chapters (Num. 3 and 4) describe in detail the furnishings of the Tabernacle that each clan is responsible for as its משמרת and עבדה during the march. We are informed in the introduction to this unit (3:5–10) that the Levites are replacing the Israelites[31] and assisting the Priests in guarding the Tabernacle (vv. 6f.; see v. 38). Significantly, in this introduction, the duty of משמרת is divided in two parts: while the camp is at rest (v. 7) and in transit (v. 8).[32]

A restatement of Levitic משמרת is found after the Korahite rebellion (Num. 18:1–7). Here Aaron is given the direct mandate by God to assign Levites to the guard duty around the Tabernacle and to assist the priests in their guard duty

---

[28] Note the synonyms used in the parallelism: מצור, מצפה and the verb ואצפה. The masculine nominal form משמר which never veers from the meaning of "guard," "custody" (e.g., Gen. 40:3f., 7, 42:17, 19; Lev. 24:12) only strengthens my case.

[29] D. Daube, *Studies in Biblical Law* (1947) 13–15, argues that the participial noun שומר was a legal term for a person entrusted with the custody and care of an object (e.g., Exod. 22:6 [whence the "bailee" of rabbinic law, M B.M. 7:8], and the work of the shepherd, Gen. 30:31; 1 Sam. 17:20, 28; Hos. 12:13; Jer. 31:9) and applied to "guarding" offices, e.g., city guard (Isa. 21:11f.); palace guard (2 Kings 11:5ff.); king's bodyguard (1 Sam. 26:15f.); and the Deity as guardian (Ps. 121:3ff.). Daube also argues that Cain's rejoinder (Gen. 4:9) imputes legal responsibility to the elder brother.

[30] See §§ 52–59.

[31] Ibn Ezra (on Num. 3:8), followed by Abarbanel (ad. loc.), argues that ושמרו משמרת should be rendered "guard *against* the Israelites," i.e., to prevent the Israelites from trespassing upon the sanctuary (so too in Num. 3:38). This enticing suggestion, however, fails to explain the previous verse (Num. 3:7) and the pericope immediately following (vv. 11–13) which stress that Levites succeed to positions formerly occupied by priests and laymen (vv. 40–43 similarly explicate the meaning of v. 38).

[32] For their translation and analysis, see The Composite, § 64 and accompanying notes.

within.[33] The general division of the guarding function—priests inside the sacred area and Levites outside[34]—also holds regarding their culpability. The Levites are responsible for trespassing by laymen (v. 23) and by Levites (v. 3*b*)—those who approach from the outside—and priests are responsible for trespassing by Levites (v. 3*b*) and priests (v. 7*a*) within. The foregoing is a brief summary of some highlights of this pregnant chapter, Numbers 18, whose details are discussed throughout this work (see the notes, supra, for references), particularly in the treatment on עבדה, §§ 54–57. The final case of שמר משמרת in P's Tabernacle texts is Numbers 31:30, 47 where we learn that it is the Levitic office of Tabernacle guards (שמרי משמרת המשכן) that has entitled them to a division of the Midianite spoils. It is thus clear that "guarding" is the only rendering for משמרת in the Priestly texts where its object is the Tabernacle.

§ 6. "*For the Lord.*" Even when the object of משמרת is the Lord, the context always involves proscriptions and taboos so that "guarding" against violation is always meant. To cite examples only from P: Leviticus 8:35 (priestly consecration);[35] 18:30 (sexual violations); 22:9 (defiled priest and his food);[36]

---

[33] The guarding of the Tabernacle proper and the courtyard altar is the exclusive responsibility of the priests (v. 5), and to neither does the Levite have access (v. 3). However, since the non-priest was admitted to the "entrance" area within the courtyard, presumably it is there where the Levite guard was brought in to assist his priestly counterpart. This is what is meant by ושמרו את משמרתך (Num. 3:7) and ושמרו את משמרתו (Num. 18:3). It is the death knell for all translations of משמרת as *Dienst* or its equivalent (see infra n. 51). If anything characterizes P it is its painstaking effort to contrast the respective duties of priests and Levites and to bar the Levites from officiating in the cult. Only משמרת as "guarding" makes sense: Levites did guard the sanctuary entrance with the priests (observe לפני, Num. 3:7*a*, 18:2*b*), but they shared nothing else! We are now able to assert that this same differentiation is attested in the Hittite cult, see §§ 47–50.

The priests, it should be noted, had no watchpost outside the sacred area. Num. 3:38 does not assign the watchposts of the priests outside the entrance, only their *residences*! (versus Haran, "Priestly Image," 222). As for שמרים משמרת המקדש (v. 38), this phrase has to be understood with the parallel שמרי משמרת הקדש for the Kohathites (v. 28). Just as the latter refers to Kohathite guarding of the sancta during the march and has nothing to do with where they camped, so the corresponding phrase for the priests merely defines their place of employment and not their encampment. See further infra n. 233 on שמרים and esp. n. 78 on מקדש.

[34] This is also the rabbinic tradition regarding the second Temple: of the twenty-four watches at the entrance to the sacred area three were occupied by the priests; the rest by the Levites, but the latter guarded from the outside; see Sifre Zuta on Num. 18:2; also Sifra Zav, Par 2:12, 3:5; M Tam 1:1f.; M Mid 1:1, 6, 9 (see Bartinoro); Sifre 116 (ed. Horovitz, p. 131).

[35] The usual translation "keeping the Lord's charge" (NJPS) is especially deficient here. The only "charge" whose violation is punished by death (v. 35*b*) is leaving the sacred area (v. 35*a*; see v. 33).

[36] See infra n. 152.

Numbers 9:19, 23 (God directs the march);[37] Numbers 18:7a (priestly taboos concerning altar and shrine);[38] Numbers 18:8 (the priestly gifts).[39] For Ezekiel, too, שמר משמרת implies guarding against sin (the expressed meaning of 48:11 and amplified in 44:14–16), and the same principle holds.[40] Thus a semantic development is seen at work whereby guarding with weapons becomes guarding by will power; and self-discipline replaces soldiery.[41]

---

[37] But not man. The key phrase על פי ה' "by Y's order" appears seven times in this pericope (vv. 18–23); see Rashbam and Nachmanides, ad loc.

[38] See § 23, table C.

[39] See K-B for correct interpretation and infra n. 68 for further discussion.

[40] Both 44:15 and 48:11 attach משמרת with "straying" (תעה); 44:16b is followed by a string of prohibitions! 40:45 implies taboos respecting the Temple and altar; 44:8 refers especially to "guarding," see below. Note also the negative implications of ומשמרת הטהרה (Neh. 12:45) and שמר משמתרו (Mal. 3:14; cf. 1:7ff., 2:2, 11f., 3:5–9). Above all, observe that משמרתי תשמר is followed by תשמר את חצרי (Zech. 3:7).

[41] שמר משמרת as "performing guard duty" will throw welcome light upon the vexing and much discussed passage of Ezek. 44:6ff. Here, we are told, the Levites will replace the foreigners in the function of שמר משמרת (vv. 8b, 14), and in v. 11, the prophet spells out precisely what he means. The exegesis of this pregnant verse is reserved for the discussion of עבדה (§ 73), and I shall record only relevant details here. The Levites are given two main functions: guarding the gates and assisting the people (not the priests!) in the preparation of the sacrifices. Essentially, then, משמרת implies guard duty, but, in addition, temple guards are expected to be helpful to the laity with their sacrifices, a matter already assumed in P (Num. 16:9b) and faithfully followed by Ezekiel (§ 73). I say "essentially" because, as will be shown (§ 73), the assistance which is specified, i.e., ritual slaughter, is a duty probably not performed by the foreigner/Levite but by the layworshipper himself. (This fact has crucial implications, see § 12.) Thus, when שמר משמרת is used to describe and sum up the functions of the foreigner/Levite (vv. 8b, 14) it must refer to their principal role as Temple guards. That aliens were used to guard the first Temple is clear from 2 Kings 11:4. (On the problem of כרת/כרי, see J. Montgomery and H. Gehman, *Kings*, ICC [1951] 85f., note on 1 Kings 1:38.) W. R. Smith, *The Old Testament in the Jewish Church* (1907) 261f. also adds 1 Kings 14:28; Zeph. 1:8f. See also H. H. Rowley, *Worship in Ancient Israel* (1967) 99f.

Moreover, as already noted, once the object of שמר משמרת is the Deity, the meaning changes to "guard the taboos." That is why the otherwise puzzling ולא שמרתם משמרת קדשי (8a) can be addressed to the people; surely, they have no cultic functions to perform! However, in allowing the foreigners to enter the sacred area (see Josh. 9:27), Israel "had not guarded my sancta." Similarly, ושמרו את משמרתי (v. 16b) does not mean that the Zadokites will henceforth perform the cultic service. Attention has not been paid to the verses which follow (14ff.). They are a string of prohibitions and should be separated from the preceding by nothing more than a colon, for they are the משמרת ה', the divine taboos.

Finally, it will be noted that the Zadokites (אשר שמרו את משמרת מקדשי) (15a) differ from both the Levites and the foreigners whose משמרת is performed במקדשי (8b, 11a). The reason for the change to the preposition ב is that Ezekiel speaks now solely of the priestly guarding, and he resorts to P's idiom (Num. 3:38) for the ancient function of the priests as guardians of the sacred area and/or sancta (for the meaning of

The need for a more literal understanding of משמרת is also valid for the idiom היה למשמרת, where, in at least two cases, it must be translated as "keep under guard" or "safeguard": the Pesach offering must be guarded during the four days that elapse between its selection and slaughter lest any accident disqualify it (Exod. 12:6).[42] Out of similar fears the ashes of the red heifer require guarding (Num. 19:9).[43]

§ 7. משמרת *in Chronicles.*[44] In Chronicles, שמר משמרת still carries the ground meaning "to guard" to judge from its use in the description of King Saul's

---

מקדש, see infra n. 78). The standard treatment of משמרת is found in H. Gese, *Der Verfassungsentwurf des Ezechiel, BHTh*, 25 (1957) 64–67; Gunneweg, 188–203; W. Zimmerli, *Ezechiel*, B.K., 13 (1967) fasc. 13–14:1125–1133.

[42] So Mek of R Simeon, ad loc.: Pes 96*a*, and see infra n. 51.

[43] E.g., M Par, ch. 9. According to early rabbinic tradition, no human guard was required over the ashes since one-third of the ashes was hermetically sealed and secreted on the Mount of Olives; Sifre Zuta, ad loc.: see also Sifre Num. 124 and H. Albeck's note on M Par 3:11 (*Commentary on Mishna*, VI, *Tohorot*, ed. Albeck-Yalon [1959] 561 [Heb.]). Tosef Par 3:14 claims it for the third of the ashes deposited in the Temple rampart. In either case, the meaning still holds: "for safeguarding."

[44] Though the semantic history of משמרת does not fall within the scope of this study the following points are relevant:

1. The progression of guarding > custody > duty/service > service unit is perfectly logical and needs no justification. The only question is where (or when) is each change attested. In my judgment, the original meanings "guarding" and "custody" (found in the earliest sources, e.g., 1 Sam. 22:23; 2 Sam. 20:3; Isa. 21:8; Hab. 2:1), merely represent a feminine form of משמר (see supra n. 28).

2. "Service"/"duty," the next meaning, is strictly the Deuteronomist's coinage (e.g., Deut. 11:1; Josh. 22:3; 1 Kings 2:3) and is elsewhere only attested in the later literature (Zech. 3:7; Mal. 3:14; Neh. 12:45; 1 Chron. 23:32; 2 Chron. 13:11, 23:6).

3. The final evolution of משמרת into "service unit" is not found in the Bible at all! As correctly observed by S. Japhet, "The Supposed Common Authorship of Chron. and Ezra–Neh. Investigated Anew," *VT* (1968) 330–371, esp. 344–348, this concept is expressed by מחלקת (found plentifully in Chronicles, but only twice in the Aramaic texts of Ez-Neh), and, though she does not investigate the usage of משמרת, I can now assert that not even once is the meaning of "service unit" attested. This holds true unequivocally for the singular משמרת, but what of the plural משמרות, uniformly rendered by all translations "service units/divisions" or the equivalent? It can be shown that in Chronicles משמרות is but the plural abstract of "duty" (see esp. 2 Chron. 8:14 where it is parallel to עבדה; also 2 Chron. 7:6, 31:16, 35:2). Only once does it refer to a service unit (1 Chron. 9:23 and possibly 1 Chron. 26:12), but here it refers to a unit of guards, in which case it is the plural of משמר and not משמרת. This state of affairs is also reflected in Ez-Neh where משמרות are "guard units" and where its singular is explicitly משמר (Neh. 7:3; see Neh. 4:3, 16, 12:25). It is, therefore, doubtful whether the remaining two instances of משמרות (Neh. 12:9, 13:30) refer to "service units" and are not the plural abstract for "duty," as evidenced everywhere else. (The masc. pl. משמריו is found once: Neh. 13:14, but its meaning is ambiguous and it is missing from the LXX). In any event, the use מחלקת instead of משמרת/משמרות in Chronicles points to the post-biblical period as the time when משמרת became the technical term for a "unit of cultic service." (See Japhet, notes on 346f. for references.)

palace (1 Chron. 12:29). The Levites, too, carry this obligation in relation to the Temple, as we read: "they spent the night round about the house of God (כי עליהם המשמרת) because they were responsible for the guard" (1 Chron. 9:27).[45] Most illuminating of all are the parallel accounts of Jehoiada's insurrection (2 Kings 11:5–9; 2 Chron. 23:4–8). The soldier-guards for young Joash in Kings are replaced by Levites in Chronicles, with the added warning: "none must enter the house of the Lord except the priests and Levitical ministrants; they may enter because they are consecrated, but all the people shall keep the Lord's taboo.[46] The Levites are to surround the king (איש וכליו בידו והבא אל הבית יומת), each one with his weapons in his hand—anyone who enters the house shall be put to death" (vv. 6–7a). The reason for the Chronicler's switch is transparent: no layman is permitted into the Temple proper.[47] That the Chronicler offers no

---

[45] The allusion to Num. 1:53 cannot be missed.

[46] The Chronicler's special pleading on behalf of the Levites has been noted by all the commentaries. However, the attempt to give legal status to his innovations needs further comment. For example, in this pericope, the Chronicler justifies the Levites' right of entry into the בית on the grounds that they are קדש whereas the people must observe the divine taboo (ישמרו משמרת ה') and stay out. However, nowhere else is the Levite called קדש! Indeed, merely by comparing the induction service of the priests (Exod. 29; Lev. 8) with the Levites' (Num. 8) one can readily see how deliberately and meticulously P refuses to utilize the root קדש in connection with the Levites. Clearly, the Chronicler has not only ignored P but defied it. (For another example, see infra n. 307.)

[47] These verses give pause because they ostensibly aver, contrary to P's system and all of Scripture, that the Levites might "enter into the house of the Lord" (בית ה'). However, this can hardly refer to the sanctuary itself because the Chronicler scrupulously keeps the Levites out in every other instance, e.g., 2 Chron. 29:16, where the priests enter the sanctuary to cleanse it and transmit the impurity to the Levites waiting in the courtyard. True, the same chapter tells us that the Levite musicians reoccupied their old stations in בית ה' (29:25), but this only requires a reevaluation of the definition or, rather, the range of the technical terms בית and היכל. It will be noted that when the Chronicler wishes to specify the sanctuary proper he uses the term היכל, *never* בית. The two are not the same, for the Temple building (בית) contained three stories of rooms on its north and south sides (1 Kings 6:5f., 10; Ezek. 41:5–11; s.v. "Temple" *IDB*, figs. 16–18, 31). Moreover, it is possible that the term בית was a collective for the entire complex of buildings reared upon the Temple mount. As in the second Temple, there were smaller structures around the courtyard at and over the gates. Thus, Uzziah's usurpation of the priestly function of offering incense took place in the היכל but as soon as he turned leprous he was banished from the בית (2 Chron. 26:16)—obviously the entire sacred area.

The account of Josiah's reform is particularly instructive. "The Book" was obviously stored in an archive room, not in the sanctuary proper (2 Kings 22:8; 2 Chron. 34:15); the people's silver donations were deposited in a treasury room (2 Kings 22:4; 2 Chron. 34:9); the sacred horses which were at the entrance of the בית are by the chamberlain's quarters, i.e., off the sacred area (2 Kings 23:11; see Montgomery's note on פרור, ICC, 539f.); indeed, the houses of the sacred-prostitutes which were "in the house of Y. where the women wove..." (v. 7) were surely not in the

Temple building but somewhere in its area. Moreover, when the narrator means the sanctuary, he writes היכל (v. 4).

The account of Manasseh's idolatry is also instructive: "he built altars in the house of the Lord" (2 Kings 21:4), and sacrificial altars had to be in the open. (Even if this verse is a gloss on v. 5 which speaks of courtyard altars [so Montgomery, ibid.], it would be a correct gloss; it may, however, refer to roof altars, see 2 Kings 23:12).

In Ezekiel, בית can also refer to the Temple area (e.g., 40:5, 42-15) as well as the Temple building, for "massive walls surrounded the courts, which were entered through imposing doorways, the whole looking like a fortress," G. A. Cooke, *Ezekiel*, ICC (1936) 430. In Ezekiel, it is once again amply clear that בית and היכל are never confused; the latter alone designates the sanctuary (41:1, 4, 15, 20, 21, 23, 25). (See infra n. 78 for the meaning of מקדש; for בית see Gese, 126f., and my critique, n. 78).

Ezekiel's broad and narrow use of בית, I suggest, provides the simplest and most satisfying answer to an old crux: that both the priests and the Levites are שמרי משמרת הבית (40:45b, 44:14). There is no longer any need to regard them as identical, i.e., that Ezekiel's Levites are none other than the non-Zedokite priests. Zimmerli, *Ezechiel* 1128ff. is surely right in defending the integrity of the priestly משמרת הבית. To his reasons I would add the incontrovertible fact that the location of the chamber of these priests is in the inner court (40:44), an area off limits to all but priests! Aided by this new understanding of משמרת (n. 41), a new explanation is at hand: The first occurrence of the idiom (40:45b) falls in the description of the Temple (chs. 40–42) where בית as *Temple building* predominates (41:5, 7, 8, 10, 13, 14, 17, 19, 26; esp. the immediate context, 40:47, 48) whereas the second instance (44:14) occurs in a pericope where בית as the *Temple area* predominates (44:5, 5, 11, 11 [v. 4?]). This view is strengthened by focusing on the two passages in question.

In 40:45f., the two priestly groups are the שמרי משמרת המזבח and the שמרי משמרת הבית. Only their guarding responsibility is referred to (see supra n. 41). The areas to be guarded correspond precisely to those explicitly mentioned in P: ושמרתם את משמרת הקדש ואת משמרת המזבח (Num. 18:5a) where קדש refers to the sanctuary, see infra n. 149. (Gunneweg's [p. 200] coupling of Ezek. 44:16 with Num. 18:5 cannot be accepted because of his misunderstanding of משמרת.) Ezekiel differs from P only in that he assigns the altar משמרת to the Zadokites, whereas we must assume that in P the priestly משמרת was handled in rotation. (Since the Zadokite identification now implies that משמרת means the full cultic control over the altar, a sense it has only in Chronicles, it is possibly an additional reason to those posited by Zimmerli, ad loc., 1131f., why 44:16b may be a late gloss. In my judgment, however, it is no *Metaste* stemming from the *Zadokidenabschnit*, 44:6ff.; rather, the latter also received the Zadokite gloss.)

If בית for the Levites means the Temple grounds, then their duties are clearly understood. For, as will be shown in the analysis of עבדה, Ezek. 44:14 is a midrash on P's identification of Levitic duties ושמרו את משמרת אהל מועד לכל עבדת האהל (Num. 18:4a). This verse immediately precedes the definition of the priestly duties (v. 5) and would indicate that Ezekiel knew this passage very well when he described his own priests and Levites (see my discussion, § 73). The point need only be made that in substituting בית for אהל Ezekiel used a precise equivalent. For just as אהל stands for the Tabernacle complex in P (see §§ 13, 15), so בית must be the Temple complex in Ezekiel.

Thus, the correct understanding of משמרת in P and Ezekiel, and the latter's use of בית for two distinct divisions of the temple area, can lead to the resolution of our crux.

Perhaps it is also of consequence that in rabbinic Hebrew both words experience a shift: היכל may mean the Temple building, and בית embraces the larger architectural complex (e.g., M Mid 4:6).

apology for turning his Levites into "Swiss guards" can only mean that he knew this to be their ancient role and it required no explanation.[48] The historic significance of this passage will engage us later. Now it is crucial to see in the Chronicler's version a corroboration of our interpretation of the existence and purpose of the Levite guard around the Tabernacle, as predicated by P. Moreover, the similarity of the instruction to the Levites והבא אל הבית יומת[49] to our formula הזר הקרב יומת cannot be overlooked. Chronicles, then, provides us with the oldest confirmation that the Priestly source conceived of the Levites as armed guards about the Tabernacle with the authority and the means to put any trespasser to death.[50]

§ 8. *Recapitulation.* We can take serious objection to the extant lexicons and translations which render every משמרת automatically by "service" or

---

In any event, in the Bible, בית means the Temple building alone or it can encompass the smaller structures in the sacred area; but it must never be confused with היכל, the sanctuary. Thus, the implications for this passage (2 Chron. 23:6ff.) would be that neither young Joash or his bodyguard, the Levites, were actually in the sanctuary, but elsewhere in the sacred area (as clearly implied by 2 Kings 11:3a).

[48] In a private communication, Père R. De Vaux suggests that the Chronicler well knew that the Levites were not armed since he had Johiada arm them (2 Chron. 23:9) "which text sneaked as a gloss in 2 Kings 11:10." This verse, I submit, must be understood in the light of a cultic tradition which underlies other verses that were before the Chronicler, viz. 1 Kings 14:26–28; 1 Sam. 17:54 (באהל ה' for באהלו); 2 Sam. 8:7–11, esp.v.1 1 (cf. 1 Chron. 18:11); 1 Kings 7:51. These texts predicate that only *consecrated* weapons were allowed within sacred precincts: the gold ones for ceremonial purposes (e.g., 1 Kings 14:28; cf. 10:5, 7), the bronze, for more practical uses when necessary. (After all, David did not hesitate to request, nor Aḥimelek to grant, a consecrated sword—for use even outside the sacred area, 1 Sam. 21:9f.) Thus, I side with J. Gray, *The Book of Kings* (1963) 517, that 2 Kings 11:10 is not a gloss from Chronicles (indeed, where else is Chronicles > Kings harmonization authenticated?), but represents an ancient cultic norm which the Chronicler faithfully copied from Kings while adding his bias that laymen could not gain entrance into the Temple building even in Joash's day. (He did not, however, explain the incongruity of excepting Joash from his rule!)

[49] For the enigmatic שדרות in the Kings parallel, see the commentaries.

[50] Even the later term משמרות still retains "guarding" as its central function. Indeed, that the Chronicler grants Levitic status to gatekeepers only makes sense on the assumption that the original gatekeepers were the Levites themselves. See J. M. Meyers, *I Chronicles* (1965) 72f., on the probable antiquity of the gatekeeping role; see also 1 Chron. 9:27 where משמרת can mean only "guard duty" (and see Neh. 4:3, 16, 7:3, 12:45 where משמרת/משמר imply guard duty). The sanctuary gatekeeper is also well known in pagan cults, an office occupied by gods as well as men (see C. H. Gordon's *Ugaritic Textbook* (1965) Glossary, s.v. ṯǵr; see also Jean-Hoftijzer, *DISO*, s.v. שער II). On the varied use of משמרת/משמר in Ezra-Nehemiah and Chronicles, see most recently, Japhet, 18:330–371, esp. 347.

"obligation" or "charge."[51] Even in some cases of משמרת ה', where these renderings have some merit, the context deals with taboos and prohibitions so that the basic idea of "keeping watch" still holds good. However, where the object of שמר משמרת is the sanctuary, as is the case with all the contexts in which the formula occurs, there can be no doubt that the Levites are meant. It is they who are the armed sentinels stationed around the Tabernacle complex[52] and it is they who carry out the sentence of הזר הקרב יומת. When we examine the historical antecedents of the Levites we shall realize that this military role assigned them should not surprise us and that it is entirely in keeping with their image in the earliest sources.[53] But before entering into historical enquiry, I must first clarify the remaining term of the formula, קרב.[54]

קרב

§ 9. *The hypothesis.* The process of defining קרב has already begun with the identification of the two other members of the formula, זר and יומת, and

---

[51] E.g., B-D-B, K-B, G-B; RSV, NJPS, SB. B. Levine, *Leshonenu* (1965) 30:2–11, esp. 9ff. equates משמרת with בקרת "inspection" (e.g., Lev. 13:36; Ezek. 34:11f. and Tanaaitic literature). His evidence is twofold, (1) rabbinic exegesis of Exod. 12:6, and (2) the Akkadian *batqa ṣabātu* in the sense of "to take care of" (*CAD*, s.v. ṣabātu 8, a), 2'b). On both counts, the demonstration must be rejected. (1) The connection of Exod. 12:6 with "inspection" (בקרת), as adduced by rabbinic sources, is purely coincidental. Since the paschal sacrifice is selected four days prior to its slaughter (for reasons that are lost to us) it is obvious that it requires inspection to fulfill the requirement that it be unblemished (v. 5). But the primary purpose of משמרת is that it remain under guard so that it can retain its unblemished status while awaiting slaughter. Moreover, the notion of "inspection" over against "guarding" would be alien to the other cases of biblical למשמרת: Aaron's rod (Num. 17:25), the manna (Exod. 16:23, 32–34), and the red heifer ashes (see § 6 and nn. 42, 43). Also, that Num. 4:32*b* cannot be adduced as proof, despite NJPS, see § 57, n. 233. (2) Akkadian *batqa ṣabātu* is incorrectly used. *CAD*'s "to take care of" means that the tenant/trustee will keep the property in good condition. Indeed, under *batqu* 3a, the citation from the same date palm text is translated "will keep . . . in good repair." In any event, the notion of "inspection" is flatly contradicted by the משמרת duties of the Kohathites over the "most sacred" cult objects including the Ark itself (Num. 3:28, 31): would they dare inspect sancta, the very sight of which, not to speak of touch, would bring instantaneous death (Num. 4:14–20)?

[52] While the priests guard only from within, and at the gate, versus Haran on Num. 3:38, "Priestly Image," 222; see n. 33, and Hittite parallels, § 48.

[53] See §§ 44–47. Guarding the sanctuary as the main Levitic office has already been noted in the early rabbinic sources, n. 35. Philo also concurs: "temple attendants who had none of these (priestly) duties but had the care and guarding of the sacred building and its contents by day and night" (*Moses*, II, 174 [Loeb VI, 535]; see *On Rewards and Punishments*, 74 [Loeb VIII, 357]).

[54] The term עבדה, like משמרת, clusters around occurrences of the formula, and is equally as important in its elucidation. However, because its study is of some length and will distract too long from the main objective, I have appended it to the main discussion, see §§ 52–75.

the related concept משמרת, within whose contexts קרב has to operate. The question is twofold: (1) Does קרב mean literally "approach" or is actual contact involved? (2) Is the act deliberate or accidental?

Rabbinic tradition unanimously avers that both contact and intention are implied by קרב: the unauthorized person presumes to usurp the functions of priests or Levites, i.e., he is an encroacher.[55] I submit that the contexts of all four occurrences of the formula support this interpretation.

§ 10. *Numbers 1:51.* This first occurrence states the removal duties of the Levites: "When the Tabernacle is to set out, the Levites shall dismantle it, and when the Tabernacle is to be pitched, the Levites shall assemble it, but any outsider הקרב shall be put to death." Interference with the Levitic office is implied, as the next verse will confirm.

§ 11. *Numbers 3:10.* In the second occurrence, the context (vv. 5–10) again defines the Levitic duties relating to the Tabernacle but concentrates upon their guard duty in camp (v. 7) and in march (v. 8).[56] The priests also are given guard duty over their priestly functions (v. 10a),[57] "but any outsider הקרב shall be put to death." When we consider that the Levitic sentries were posted around the Tabernacle complex (and around the sacred objects when they were transported) then הקרב can hardly mean "approach." The Levites are not standing on holy ground; they are stationed around the sacred area. Moreover, according to the Priestly system, there is no prohibition against contact with the person of the Levite or priest.[58] Thus, I would have to infer that קרב goes beyond "approach" and even "contact" but implies a deliberate attempt to break through the protective cordons to interfere with the functions of the clergy, i.e., "encroach." My suspicions are strengthened by the verses that follow:

§ 12. *Numbers 3:38.* At the third occurrence of the formula the priests also take up guard duty at the entrance, "keeping guard[59] over the sacred area,[60] a guard duty on behalf of the Israelites; but the stranger הקרב shall be put to death." This passage demonstrates beyond doubt that קרב cannot take the literal meaning of "approach." For according to P's own system, the layman had access to a corridor within the sanctuary enclosure, termed פתח אהל מועד, which extended

---

[55] Sifre Num. 116 (ed. S. Horovitz, 134); Sanh 83b; see M Sanh 9:6; Sifre Zuta on Num. 18:3, 7 (ed. Horovitz, 291, 293). Also NJPS.

[56] See The Composite, § 64, ad loc., and accompanying notes.

[57] Comp. Num. 18:7 and its discussion, § 13.

[58] Only Ezekiel enjoins the priest from contact with laity (44:19), but only while he wears his sacred vestments, i.e., he is officiating at the altar but not performing guard duty (cf. Num. 18:4b).

[59] Following Haran's astute observation; see n. 233 for reference and discussion.

[60] Or "sacred objects," but not "sanctuary," see infra n. 78. That the priests guard within the sacred area exclusively, see supra n. 33.

between the enclosure gate and the courtyard altar.[61] Here the layman was directed to perform certain vital acts with his animal oblation, in preparation for the altar ritual of the priest, namely: the presentation, hand-laying rite, slaughter, and flaying of the animal (e.g., Lev. 1:3–6); also in that area, the people could assemble as spectators as well as participants (e.g., Lev. 8:3f., 9:5). Thus the warning of Numbers 3:38 can hardly be directed against the layman who merely "approaches" the priestly cordon. Since passage through the guards into the enclosure is a guaranteed right for the laity, the action of קרב can only refer to a deliberate attempt to exceed one's privileges, i.e., if the layman is "encroaching."[62]

§ 13. *Numbers 18:7.* This verse, the fourth occurrence of the formula, is part of a long unit which begins with the plague inflicted upon Israel in the wake of the Korahite rebellion (Num. 16f., see esp. 16:35, 17:11–15), continues with the panicky outcry of the Israelites that "all who merely seek access to the Lord's Tabernacle must die" (17:28), and concludes with the antidote to the people's fears (18:1–24, esp. v. 1–7, 21–23). The immediate context of the formula is similar to Numbers 3:10 (see supra), specifying the guard duty of the priests but adding the significant terminology of priestly עבדה.[63] The inference is quite plausible that הזר הקרב is the unauthorized usurper of priestly functions.

Plausibility becomes probability when we find the same apposition of קרב and עבדה in 18:22f.: "Henceforth, Israelites shall not יקרבו אל the Tent of Meeting to incur mortal guilt; only Levites shall perform the labor (ועבד . . . עבדת) of the Tent of Meeting."[64] Again, the translation "approach" would be incorrect since, as noted above, the layman did have access into part of the sacred area. The apposition of עבדה, moreover, makes it certain that the notion of "accidental" is also precluded. The text blares forth its message: the Levites shall permanently replace the Israelites in the Tabernacle (reiterated frequently: Num. 3:7f., 11–13, 41, 45, 8:14–19, 16:9); only Levites shall perform עבדה. Thus, I am forced to conclude that הזר הקרב is one who may not perform עבדה. He is the "encroacher."

§ 14. *Korah.* Further corroboration appears in the long unit on Korah's rebellion (Num. 16–18). Korah and his followers did not die because they tres-

---

[61] See M Kel 1:8; Sifre Zuta (on Num. 5:2), and Haran's discussion, "Priestly Image," 224 and *Sefer Segal*, 7f. (Heb.). More study is still required.

[62] Snijders, 143, infers from Num. 1:53 that Israelites who approached the Tabernacle area risked death by God. His misreading of קרב, יומת and the Korah pericope— esp. Num. 18:22—leads him to conjecture (with J. Pedersen) that the entire account of the Levitic encampment around the Tabernacle was a fiction invented by P (in the post-exilic age) to remove the laity from any access to the sacred area! See further infra n. 83.

[63] See §§ 57–75 and my exegesis of Num. 18:7, § 64, n. 275.

[64] The fuller implications of Num. 18:22f. are discussed in §§ 20–29. See also the Composite, § 64, ad loc. and accompanying notes.

passed into areas forbidden to them! The text clearly states they remained "at the entrance to the Tent of Meeting" (16:18f.)—an area permitted to all laymen (see supra). Hence, their sin was not in "approaching" the sancta but in their attempt to encroach upon the priestly function of offering incense. The summation in the text makes this clear: "so that an outsider who is not of Aaron's seed will not presume (יקרב) to offer incense before the Lord" (17:5).[65] It is not where they ventured to go but what they ventured to do that condemned Korah and his cohorts. Thus, קרב cannot mean "approach" or any other word which connotes physical distance; it can only refer to the act of usurpation or "encroachment."

§ 15. *The clarification of* קרב. It is now possible to see the entire Korah episode in a new light: The prescriptions of Numbers 18:1–7 are brought in answer to the people's outcry over the plague (17:11–15). In their panic, they refuse to have anything to do with the Tabernacle (17:28).[66] How does this answer alleviate their fears? It is usually understood as the call for a Levitic and priestly buffer zone to prevent Korahite-type transgressions. This explanation will not do. First, Levite guard duty around the sanctuary has already been established (Num. 1:53), and in almost identical phraseology (Num. 3:6–8). Second, the mere existence of watchmen would not be enough to calm this panic-stricken people. For no matter how well the clergy performed their watch, there would always be the possibility of another Korah breaking through and another plague breaking out. Indeed, since Korah was a Levite, the possibility existed that the encroachment might stem from the Levitic guard itself!

The answer of Numbers 18:1–7 is no mere rewording of the previously given formation of sanctuary guards[67] but contains the novel pronouncement, the hitherto unexpressed and unanticipated dictum, that priests and Levites will bear all the guilt for future encroachments, lay and clerical alike (18:1, 3, 23). Indeed, it is only because guard duty is henceforth fraught with mortal risk that priests and Levites are each assigned special emoluments as compensation.[68] Moreover, since the Levites, who live and work in close range of the sancta,[69] have more opportunities and temptations for encroachment than the laity, a special warning is directed to them: "they shall have no access (יקרבו) to the

---

[65] NJPS, correctly.

[66] This is the meaning of the two consecutive הקרב's and is not limited to "approach"; see the discussion of Korah's sin, supra.

[67] See Gray, ICC; A. M. McNeile, Cambridge, ad loc.

[68] It is expressly stated so for the Levites (18:23a) but not for the priests. However, משמרת תרומתי (18:8) may imply the priests' reward for their guarding risks; see infra n. 275.

[69] See Num. 16:9 and The Composite § 64 and n. 272 for P's high regard for the Levitic office.

furnishings of the sanctuary[70] or to the altar" (v. 3*b*). Conversely, the priests are also warned: "and the outsider shall not be associated (יקרב) with you" (v. 4*b*). If there were any possibility left that קרב means "approach," the latter citation has demolished it; for there is no prohibition to be in the presence of priests or even, in P, to touch one.[71]

Thus it is clear from all the four contexts in which the formula falls that קרב can mean only "encroach." Having defined all the terms, it is now possible to render the formula in full: הזר הקרב יומת "the unauthorized encroacher shall be put to death."

§ 16. *The principle of intention.* I am, therefore, in full agreement with the rabbinic exegesis: קרב לעבדה, i.e., that קרב of the formula refers to encroachment. But here a demurrer must be entered. We are not to think that a straying Israelite who brushes against a "most sacred" object incurs no penalty. For if the Kohathites are struck down for accidentally touching covered sancta (Num. 4:15) or seeing uncovered ones (Num. 4:20), all the more so for less privileged Israelites. In this regard, P accords completely with the historical sources that the principle of intention plays no part in violations of sacred taboos, e.g., Uzzah's touching the Ark (2 Sam. 6:6f.) and the Beth Shemeshites' viewing of it (1 Sam. 6:19) were not deliberate acts. P, moreover, goes beyond the evidence of the narratives in extending this taboo to all the cult objects[72] and not just to the Ark: the unconsecrated who make contact with them will die.[73]

At the beginning of this study of קרב (§ 9) I asked: Is the formula limited to deliberate acts, as posited by the Sages? From the foregoing, the answer would seem to be in the negative. However, this is not so. The formula does not generalize all contacts with "the most sacred"; it specifies only those contacts which are punishable by יומת, death by the sacred guards. Scanning the four loci in which the formula occurs shows it is, in each instance, directed against Israelites and Levites who attempt to break through the protective cordons placed around the sancta, both in camp and in transit. Their act is deliberate;

---

[70] It is also possible to translate Num. 18:4*b*, 5 as follows: "The outsider shall not intrude upon you as you guard over the sanctuary (following syntax of NJPS). Thus (*waw* of conclusion, see v. 22), wrath shall never again strike the Israelites." V. 5*b* would, then, serve as a conclusion to vv. 1–5, proclaiming the new doctrine of the clergy's responsibility for all encroachments upon the sanctuary.

[71] For the exception of Ezekiel, see supra n. 58.

[72] I avoid the term "most sacred objects" advisedly. For P does allow the Merarites and Gershonites to handle the frame and coverings of the Tabernacle with impunity, even though technically they are also "most sacred" (cf. Exod. 30:26*a*, 29, 40:9). Indeed among the cult objects themselves, there are distinctions, e.g., the sancta within the Tent are of higher sanctity than the outside altar; but this distinction, we shall see, is of moment only to disqualified priests (§§ 37–41) and not to the laity.

[73] Rabbinic Judaism, it should be noted, does introduce the principle of intention in contacts with the most sacred, see n. 162.

they have not as yet made contact with the sancta, but that is their intent; and they must be cut down. Thus קרב *in the formula* indeed posits intention, and it has nothing to do with the axiom assumed by all the sources—that contact with the most sacred, be it even accidental, is a lethal sin.

Herein lies still another undergirding principle. יומת is applied *only* for encroachment, i.e., if the warning of the guard goes unheeded and the encroacher persists in his trespass. When, however, the sancta are contacted accidentally, we never hear of יומת but only of ימות: God punishes the malefactor, He alone.[74]

§ 17. *Why* יומת. Only now is it possible to grapple with the question which derived from the study of יומת (§ 3), why death by man is decreed for sanctuary encroachment but for no other cultic sin. Indeed, now that קרב has been defined as "encroachment," implying deliberate defiance of the law, the difficulty is even compounded. For death by God is the sentence peremptorily imposed for all wilful violations of God's commandments (Num. 15:30f.). Could there be imagined any more brazen defiance of God than by encroachment upon His sancta? Why then is the slaying delegated to man? The answer lies in the consequences of קרב. Illicit contact with the holy produces divine wrath (קצף) or plague (נגף) which not only strikes down the sinner but engulfs his community.[75] That is why the establishment of the Levite guard is often coupled with the motive clause: "that wrath shall no longer strike the Israelites" (Num. 1:53, 18:5; see 8:19). It is crucial that the intruder be stopped before he carries out the encroachment and triggers the deadly consequences. The sacerdotal guards must cut down the criminal before God cuts down everyone else!

§ 18. *The wrong principle.* Thus, the right to kill with which the sanctuary guards are empowered is not to be confused with the legal category of capital punishments, whereby death is set as just payment for the crime. The action of the guards has nothing to do with justice. The proper category which describes their function goes back to the root purpose of their guarding: שמר משמרת as a military category. The encroacher is the enemy who has it in his power to slay all of Israel. Since he is bent on encroachment, words will not dissuade him; in

---

[74] P's principle that crimes against the sanctuary are not for man to punish has consequences for biblical religion, and even for Judaism itself; but it is not within my scope to pursue them. They are reserved for a study of the *ḥaṭṭ'āṭ* sacrifice, now in preparation.

[75] קצף/נגף is technically not a legal penalty; it is a reflex action, an outburst of the Deity resulting from egregious evil. It follows in the wake of idolatry (e.g., Num. 25:9, 18f., 31:16; see Josh. 22:17; Ps. 106:29); rebellion (Num. 17:11–15, 27f.; Josh. 22:20); war census (Exod. 30:12; 1 Chron. 27:24; see 2 Sam. 24, esp. vv. 21, 25; 1 Chron. 21:14, 22). It is also the inevitable outcome of illicit contact with sancta (Num. 1:53, 18:5; see I Sam. 4:17, 6:4, 19; see also infra n. 141). However, P effectively restricts the outbreak of divine קצף/נגף for encroachment upon sancta to the clergy alone; see §§ 17, 24.

fact, to argue is to increase the danger; he must be struck down in his tracks. The implications of this vital point will be fully assessed later (§ 24). In the meantime let it suffice to conclude that the formula הזר הקרב יומת has all along been an illusory exception to the confirmed rule that God Himself exacts the death penalty for cultic crimes. In reality, it only reinforces the rule, since it states: unless the encroacher is slain, the Deity is sure to exercise His wrath.[76]

§ 19. *Why* יומת. The last instance of the formula occurs in a pericope (18:1–24) which is no pointless repetition of previous statements of the guarding function of the clergy but declares that henceforth Levites and priests will be responsible for lay encroachment. This far-reaching innovation, I submit, only increases the urgency for the guards to kill the encroacher (see § 24). Moreover, this explains why twice, and twice only, the layman's encroachment is punishable by ימות and not by יומת, i.e., by God and not by man (Num. 17:28, 18:22: see supra table B8). The two occurrences form the framework of a distinct literary unit which cites an illness and its remedy. The second verse (18:22) is the prescription for the pathology of the first (17:28) and therefore uses the same vocabulary. It tells us that the people no longer have to fear that they will perish with the encroacher. Henceforth, only the Levites will be punished. This interpretation will yield greater fruit, but it must await the exegesis of the key phrase והם ישאו עונם (18:23).

והם ישאו עונם

§ 20. *The problem.* As a consequence of the Korahite plague the people develop a phobia towards the Tabernacle: they will not come near it (Num.

---

[76] An ostensibly different deduction was made from tables A and B (n. 26): the clergy's sins in the sanctuary, in contradiction to the layman's, are punished by God, not by man—including their encroachment (Num. 18:3; see table B7)! But if tampering with sancta can incite divine wrath upon the community, why are not the clerical offenders put to death immediately by man? The answer is most realistic: who will execute the death sentence? The encroacher himself is a guard and he is armed! Moreover, the clergy operate in the vicinity of the sancta, and could not be stopped in time. This not only holds true for the priests who guard the most sacred objects in the Tabernacle (and have access to the forbidden inner sanctum [18:7; Lev. 16:2] or, if disqualified, still may remain in the courtyard [see §§ 39–41]) but also for the Levites who carry and guard the sancta during the march (see §§ 54–59). Who, for example, could stop a Kohathite from touching the object he carries (see Num. 4:15)? Thus, as a matter of principle, where man is incapable of executing the death penalty imposed for offending the Deity, He Himself will intervene (see supra nn. 8 and 10 on כרת/מות). Num. 18:3, however, carries a new message. It informs us that if priests do not succeed in stopping a Levite encroacher (who is, after all, a זר), then the entire Levite and priestly guard is liable to death: the Levites, so that the encroacher will think twice before jeopardizing his family and tribe; the priests, so that they will guard more effectively. This pregnant verse is, furthermore, to be seen from the perspective of the entire pericope, and represents an aspect of the new shift of responsibility for

17:27–28). To allay their fright, assurance is given them that henceforth priests and Levites *alone* will share the fate of the encroacher (Num. 18:1–7); there will be no more indiscriminate mass repercussions (Num. 18:22f.). This innovation[77] is semantically highlighted by the threefold use of the idiom נשא עון (vv. 1, 1, 23); a closer look at the entire pericope is therefore indicated.

Liability for sacred objects[78] is divided into three groupings: priests and

---

sanctuary encroachment: Levites on behalf of laymen, priests and Levites for Levites, and priests for themselves. See § 23, table C, and the explication in the accompanying notes.

[77] No longer must we share the puzzlement of the commentators why the Levitic role as sanctuary guards, already stated (Num. 1:53, 3:6–8), is allegedly repeated aimlessly in ch. 18.

[78] So המקדש (18:1) must be understood. See also Num. 10:21 "the Kohathites who carried the sacred objects (המקדש)" where any other interpretation is precluded. (B. D. Eerdman's "The Composition of Numbers," *OTS* [1949] 6:101–216, esp. 127, excludes the Ark on the presupposition that it was moved to the front to lead the Wilderness march. But this is the view of JE not P.)

Indeed, מקדש *in P never means the sanctuary building*. It either refers to "the sacred area," the holy place (Lev. 12:4, 16:33, 20:3, 21:12, 12, 26:2 = 19:30; Num. 19:20) or to "the sacred objects," the sancta (Lev. 21:23, 26:31; Num. 3:38, 10:21, 18:1). Of the latter group, especially compelling are Num. 10:21, supra; Lev. 21:23, where the impaired priest is not prohibited from the sacred area but from the sancta (see previous verse: also note the plural and see § 38); and Lev. 26:31, where the verb "desolate" implies an object (i.e., "your sancta"), not an area (the plural no longer has to be taken as evidence for multiple sanctuaries!). The one possible exception is Exod. 25:8, "make Me a sanctuary," but from the following verse, מקדש is defined as המשכן ואת . . . כל כליו, "the Tabernacle and all its furnishings," i.e., all the objects of the sacred area of which the Tabernacle is but one. Indeed, the full name of the Jerusalem Temple predicates my conclusions: בית המקדש means "the house of the sancta" or "the house of the sacred area" (see 1 Chron. 28:10).

It should also be noted that Ezekiel, just like P, never uses מקדש for the sanctuary building; in all twenty-seven occurrences, of the term, it refers to "the sacred precincts." I disagree emphatically with Gese, 126f., followed by Gunneweg, 193f., that in the "Sadoquidenschicht" (44:6ff.), מקדש is restricted to the sanctuary building. If this were true, foreigners would hitherto have been allowed entry into the shrine (vv. 7–9), an unlikely possibility (note how carefully v. 7 writes בהקריבכם, referring to the Israelites whereas the נכר are only in the third person; also see supra n. 41 on משמרת), and the Levites would, henceforth, assist inside the shrine (v. 11a), a privilege denied to them by P or history (for Ezekiel's verifiable concession to the Levites, see § 73). Moreover, מקדש as "Temple precincts" now illumines the entire pericope in a new light:

1. Foreigners are banned from the entire sacred area which corresponds with the reality of the Herodian temple. (The origin of the latter's warning inscriptions may thus be much earlier than posited by the critics; see E. J. Bickerman, "Une proclamation Sélucide relative au Temple de Jérusalem," *Syria* [1947] 25:69–85; idem, "The Warning Inscriptions of Herod's Temple," *JQR* [1947] 37:387–405.)

2. Now it is understandable why the Israelites—the true culprits (vv. 6–8)—are not themselves barred from the מקדש. For in Ezekiel's temple they continue to have access to the outer court (e.g., 46:3, 9) which is also sacred (note the expression המקדש החיצון—at the head of this chapter, 44:1!).

Kohathites are responsible for Israelite encroachment (v. 1*a*);[79] priests and Levites for Levitic encroachment (v. 3); and priests for priestly encroachment (v. 1*b*).[80] This new alignment of responsibility is the innovation of this unit;[81] it insures that "wrath will no longer (עוד) strike the Israelites" (v. 5*b*).[82] However, one group is still unaccounted for: the opening verses specify the liability of priests and Kohathites for Israelite encroachment. Is there no liability borne by the Levitic tribe as a whole? This missing group is found in the concluding section of the pericope (vv. 21–23) which speaks of the dues accruing to the Levites for their labor. The reason for this puzzling displacement will engage us presently. In the meantime let us focus on the statement of the new Levitic responsibility: "The Israelites shall no longer[83] incur mortal guilt by encroaching upon the Tent of Meeting. Only the Levites shall perform the labor of the

---

3. The Levites are, of course, also eligible to be in the מקדש not just in the outer court but in the inner gate (for the implications of this concession see § 73 and n. 315)

4. The sequence described in v. 16*a* makes sense: the priests must enter the sacred area before they reach the altar.

5. שמרו את משמרת מקדשי (v. 15*a*) is a quotation from P (Num. 3:38); just as it means "sacred area" there (infra n. 149, but see supra n. 60), it means that here (see n. 44 for details).

6. לשרת את הבית is elsewhere explained as cooking the people's well-being sacrifice (46:24). This takes place in the outer court and is still called במקדשי (see further § 73).

However, just as בית is capable of meaning both the temple area and the temple building (see Gunneweg, 193f., and infra n. 47), so the possibility must be entertained that מקדש is capable of the more restricted meaning of the sacred area reserved exclusively for the priests, i.e., the 100 × 100 cubit inner court (e.g., 45:18–20 where the purification ritual for the מקדש/בית includes the inner gates! This might also explain the priestly title משרתי המקדש, 45:4). In any event, מקדש in Ezekiel, as in P, can never mean just the sanctuary building.

[79] While priests alone guard the most sacred objects during the encampment (Num. 3:38, 18:5*a*), the Kohathites guard them in transit (4:4–15). That ובית אביך means literally "your father's house" (Aaron's clan is the Kohathites) is confirmed by particle וגם (v. 2) which clearly distinguishes the clan from the tribe.

[80] See 3:10*a* and my discussion of 18:17, infra n. 275.

[81] Bechor Shor correctly, in my opinion, admonishes Rashbam for claiming as the innovation of the pericope the penalty of death for encroachment (v. 8*b*), since it (my formula) has previously appeared thrice. He, in turn, favors v. 3 as the innovation, i.e., the priests are henceforth responsible for future Levite (Korahite) encroachments. Thus, Bechor Shor has latched on to the correct governing principle but he misses the main area of its application: Levitic culpability for lay encroachment.

[82] See supra n. 70 for a possible rendering of vv. 4*b*–5.

[83] Snijders, 154, follows J. Pedersen, *Israel* iii–iv (1940) 280 that "the expression 'no longer' which strictly speaking makes no sense in this context shows that the person who formulated the law was aware he was putting forward a new demand." This strange view is forced upon these two scholars by their exegesis of 18:22, "the Israelites shall no longer approach the tent . . ." which flatly contradicts P's explicit permission for the laity to enter the sacred enclosure with their offerings. However, our newly won understanding of קרב leads to a different rendering: "the Israelites

Tent of Meeting והם ישאו עונם and *they* shall bear *their* guilt" (Num. 18:22, 23a). What are the antecedents of "they" and "their"? There are three possibilities: either both pronouns stand for the Israelites, both for the Levites, or the first for Levites and the second for the Israelites.[84] I shall discuss them seriatim:

§ 21. *Solution 1.* "And they (the Israelites) shall bear their (own) guilt." This interpretation is currently in vogue.[85] Favoring it are the emphatic, otherwise superfluous, pronouns הוא and הם (v. 23). Being of different number, they ostensibly contrast with each other, and the verse means: since he, the Levite, is to perform the sacred labor, all others (i.e., Israelites) will incur blame (i.e., for attempting the same).

Weighty difficulties do not allow this interpretation to stay afloat. "Others" is an unusual rendering for הם; and even if allowed, its antecedent can hardly be the Israelites (v. 22) since the pronoun הוא, referring to the Levites, disrupts the connection. More decisively, this interpretation vitiates and contradicts the innovation which the pericope has painstakingly expounded—that the Levites and priests are assuming the culpability for the laity's sins in the Tabernacle. It would indeed be of small comfort to the panicky Israelites that in approaching the Tabernacle they are once again in peril!

§ 22. *Resolving the subject.* I must, therefore, rule out the Israelites as the antecedent of הם but stake a claim in favor of the Levites, despite the result that the Levites are referred to by a singular and plural pronoun, הוא and הם, in the same verse. Upon examination, the grammatical problem proves nonexistent. First, the alternation of singular and plural is a frequently attested phenomenon in the Priestly texts.[86] Second, the Levites occur only in the plural in the surrounding verses (vv. 21, 23b, 24) and are once actually referred to by the same pronoun הם (v. 21). Third, it is now explained why the following verbal clause (ובתוך בני ישראל לא ינחלו נחלה) has no separate subject: it needs none; it is governed by הם, the Levites. Fourth, the change of number can now be explained; in fact, the text could not have been written differently. The change underscores the very

---

shall no longer bear mortal guilt by encroaching upon the Tent. . . ." Encroachment is prohibited, not approach. Moreover, this verse cannot be a condemnation and punishment of the laity; 18:22 is an antidote to 17:28, a balm and not a rebuke. M. Haran's notion on this same point is discussed within the context of a larger critique in n. 211 infra.

[84] Theoretically, there is a fourth possibility: the first pronoun is the Levites; the second, the Israelites; but it is patently absurd.

[85] E.g., NJPS following Ehrlich.

[86] E.g., Num. 5:6f., 6:20, 18:4. The assumption that a change in number is indisputable evidence of a composite text still informs recent commentaries (e.g., Noth and Elliger on *Leviticus*).

point of the pericope: all the Levites (הם) are henceforth to bear the guilt of the individual Levite (הוא).[87]

§ 23. *Resolving the pericope.* Fifth, with the recovery of the meaning of this passage, the logical structure of the entire pericope is fully discernible. A hierarchy of responsibility is presented in vv. 1–7: priests and Kohathites are liable for incursions upon the most sacred objects (v. 1a) and the priests for their priesthood (v. 1b), in regard to the adytum and altar (7a). The Levites have also been mentioned (vv. 2, 3a) and have been declared liable for their personal encroachment upon priestly functions (v. 3b). However, the vital information that all the Levites are answerable for lay encroachment is lacking here; indeed, the telltale idiom, נשא עון, is conspicuously missing for the Levites. We find it only at the end of the unit (v. 23). Why has it been displaced? The text itself provides the answer: the announcement of the Levites' culpability awaits the itemization of their dues in order to teach that the largesse of tithes is granted them as a reward (שכר, v. 31) for the mortal risk attending their labors (חלף עבדתם) in the sanctuary (vv. 21b, 31b).[88] The resultant scheme emerges:

TABLE C

Sacral Responsibility in the Tabernacle (Num. 18:1–24)

Verse	Sacred Class	Responsible for:	Against the Encroachment of:
1, 7a(3:10a)	Priests	Most sacred objects[89]	Disqualified priests[90]
3	Priests and Levites	Most sacred objects (at rest)[91]	Levites[92]
1a(4:17ff.)	Kohathites	Most sacred objects (in transit)	Israelites
22, 23	Levites	Sanctuary, as a whole	Israelites

[87] The literary critics have been asking the wrong question. The problem is not why הם follows הלוי, but why, in a unit where the Levites occur only in the plural, is there an abrupt change to הלוי in the singular? That this startling alteration can only be deliberate is underscored by the addition of the emphatic pronoun הוא; it is the main point of the entire pericope: "each of the Levites shall perform the labor of the Tent of Meeting but all of them shall bear their guilt."

[88] Strictly speaking, the tithe is a quantitatively disproportionate return: Levi, one of thirteen in tribes, receives one of ten in produce. The added 20 percent (actually 23 percent) may be attributed to the mortal hazards in guarding the sanctuary. Indeed, since 20 percent is the standard fine for tampering with sancta (see Lev. 5:14ff.; Num. 5:5–8), is it coincidental that we meet a comparable figure here?

[89] Especially, the altar and adytum (7a). For the specific meaning, see § 13 and infra n. 146.

[90] See §§ 37–40.

[91] Priests have added responsibility for Israel's sacred gifts (8a; Lev. 22:9).

[92] See supra n. 76 on Num. 18:3.

§ 24. *Resolving the formula.* Finally, the establishment of a scale of clerical responsibility for the Tabernacle leads to further clarification of the formula הזר הקרב יומת. For only now can we understand the urgency of יומת, why the sanctuary guards are given the power to strike down all encroachers on the spot. The wrath of God kindled by the offender no longer vents itself upon the people but strikes down the Levites. No wonder the Sanctuary guards are armed; their lives are at stake! The encroacher is, in effect, their murderer, and they kill him in self-defense.[93]

Moreover, as shown by Table C, there exists a hierarchy in clerical responsibility. When a single Levite (another Korah) encroaches upon the sancta, all the Levites and all the priests are held responsible, i.e., the sanctuary guards as a body incur the blame. But when the encroacher is an Israelite, the Levites alone suffer. The relationships are clear: priests must guard against Levites and Levites against Israelites. And logically so. The Levite encroacher has only the priestly guard to overcome, for the latter alone stands between him and the most sacred objects (18:5a). The Israelite encroacher, on the other hand, should be thwarted by the Levite cordon about the sanctuary. Thus, the gradations of responsibility are in accordance with physical realities—the actual distribution of the sanctuary guards.

§ 25. *Resolving the object.* Now for the identity of the pronominal suffix of עונם: does it refer to the Levites or the Israelites? Since both parties can be guilty, the layman for encroaching and the Levite for negligent guarding, does it matter, in the long run, who will be labeled with the guilt? Examination of the alternatives reveals there is a great deal at stake.

§ 26. *Two more solutions.* Solution 2: "And they (the Levites) shall bear their (own) guilt." This is the traditional exegesis.[94] The usage is standard for P.[95] Its meaning would be unambiguous and fully consonant with the context. Blame for lay encroachment is thus emphatically placed at the door of the negligent Levite guards. This interpretation is perfectly acceptable, but there is another.

Solution 3: "And they (the Levites) shall bear their (the Israelites') guilt."[96] Grammatically, this interpretation is also sound; indeed, the closest named antecedent in the plural for the pronominal suffix is the Israelites of the previous

---

[93] I am grateful to M. Greenberg for pointing out, in a private communication, that Ezek. 3:20 is clearly influenced by this concept of P; punishment is administered both to the sinner and the negligent lookout.

[94] E.g., Versions, Rabbis; KJV, SB, JPS.

[95] Lev. 5:1, 17:16, 20:17; Num. 5:31. The same plural suffix occurs in Lev. 20:19 (cf. v. 20). See also the parallel idiom נשא חטא, Lev. 24:15; Num. 9:13, and in the plural Lev. 20:20.

[96] To my knowledge, Rashi is the sole commentator who adopts this view.

verse (18:22). What now of the usage? Do we have instances of this idiom where the subject and object differ, i.e., where one party bears the guilt of a second party? The case of vows should suffice: ונשא את עונה "He (the husband) shall bear her guilt" (Num. 30:16).[97] Thus we have philological and legal attestation for a principle of vicarious culpability.

§ 27. *A new verse.* Which of the two interpretations is more acceptable? A new verse (Num. 8:19), paralleling the original passage in structure and style, forces a decision. I shall set the matching phrases side by side:

Num. 18:22f.		Num. 8:19	
ועבד הלוי הוא את עבדת אהל מועד	23aα	ואתנה אח הלוים ... לעבד את עבדת	19aα
		ב''י באהל מועד	
והם ישאו עונם	23aβ	לכפר על בני ישראל	19aβ
ולא יקרבו עוד בני ישראל אל אהל	22	ולא יהיה בבני ישראל נגף בגשת	19b
מוער לשאת חטא למות		בני ישראל אל הקרש	

The parallelism of the first and third lines is patently clear;[98] it provides the grounds for assuming that the second line across is also in parallel, i.e., that והם ישאו עונם can be explained by לכפר על בני ישראל or, better, that they throw light upon each other. Numbers 8:19 cannot imply that the Levites will perform the *kippur* ritual in the sanctuary,[99] a prerogative exclusively assigned to the priesthood. Nor is *kippur* to be understood figuratively, so that Levites "guard against sins being committed ... by keeping Israelites away from the sanctuary."[100]

§ 28. *The Levites' kippur.* Kippur as a Levitic function is clarified by the context: the ordination service of the Levites. After the Levites are purified (8:5f.), the Israelites lay their hands upon the Levites' heads (v. 10), and Aaron performs the lifting ceremonial with them (v. 11; see vv. 13, 15, 21). I shall not enter into an analysis of these two basic but abstruse rites[101] but utilize only the

---

[97] See also Ezek. 4:4. Since Ezekiel is influenced by P (see supra n. 25), it is clear that P must also be the source of the vicarious suffering of Isaiah's servant (Isa. 53:4a, 5, 11b, 12). These instances are overlooked by Ehrlich, *Randglossen* (on Num. 18:23).

[98] A consequence is that Num. 8:19b must be rendered: "so that there shall be no plague upon the Israelites when the Israelites encroach (בגשת) upon the sanctuary." The structure of בגשת is identical with בהרימכם in Num. 18:32a, "when you remove the best part you will incur no guilt." For נגש = קרב, see § 33.

[99] Cazelle's argument (SB, ad loc.) that "the Priests require the aid of the Levites" will not do. *Kippur* rites require access to the altars (inner and outer), which the Levites are forbidden to have (e.g., Num. 18:3).

[100] Greenstone, and so Gray, ad loc. But there is no basis for a figurative, metaphoric use of כפר in P. See further infra n. 110.

[101] The reader may provisionally be referred to: A. Vincent, "Les rites du balancement (tenoûphâh) et du prélèvement (teroûmâh) dans le sacrifice de communion de l'Ancien Testament," *Mélanges Syriens offerts à R. Dussaud* I (1939) 267–272; G. R. Driver, "Three Technical Terms in the Pentateuch," *JSS* (1956) 1:97–105.

unambiguous data of the ritual procedure relevant for our discussion: These two rites are elsewhere reserved exclusively for animal offerings and are never used with humans.[102] The Levites are the sole exception to the rule because they are literally sacrifices brought by the Israelites. In the case of the תנופה, the text is explicit: the Levites are "a wave offering to the Lord from the Israelites."[103] The סמיכה ritual is even more instructive. The Israelites lay their hands upon the Levites just as worshippers do upon their animals[104] and, indeed, as the Levites themselves do upon the offerings which they bring. Note the parallelism:

והלוים יסמכו את ידיהם על ראש הפרים ... לכפר על הלוים　　　(v. 12)

וסמכו בני ישראל את ידיהם על הלוים ... ולכפר על בני ישראל　　(vv. 10, 19)

על, as the preposition of כפר (pi) and followed by a human object, always means "on behalf of."[105] Thus, just as the bulls are the *kippur* on behalf of the Levites, so the Levites are the *kippur* on behalf of the Israelites. This equation is important. It shows that לכפר which elsewhere, when the priest is the subject, means "to perform the rite of *kippur*," here, when the subject is the sacrifice, and in this case, the Levites, can mean only "to be the means of *kippur*."[106] Thus, the Levites do not perform *kippur*; rather, *kippur* is performed with them.[107]

What is the nature of this Levitic *kippur*? The analogy with sacrifices can be pursued no further since the Levites are patently not offered up on the altar. The extra-sacrificial *kippur* provides assistance, of which the most helpful are the

---

[102] The priests are clearly not "waved" as part of their induction rites. והנפת אתם (Exod. 29:24; Lev. 8:27) refers solely to the offerings placed in their hands. Any doubt on that score is settled by the case of the Nazirite (Num. 6:19f.). The purpose of placing the portions for waving into their offerer's hands is to signify that these portions belong to their bearer, i.e., the one on whose behalf the priest will perform the ceremony of waving. (The rabbinic tradition that the priest places his hands under the offerer's laden hands and then "waves" them may be correct. No clearer designation of ownership could be devised.) As for סמיכה, the examples of Joshua (Num. 27:18) and the blasphemer (Lev. 24:14) are not analogous. Neither the manner nor the purpose of their handlaying corresponds to ours, but this distinction will have to await separate treatment.

[103] The Levites are dedicated, "assigned" (נתן), not consecrated (קדש) by their ordination. Indeed, nowhere in P is the root קדש used in connection with the Levites. This distinction is deliberate. Consecration, performed by anointment (Exod. 29; Lev. 8), entitles the recipient to have access to sancta. This crucial difference is missed by Speiser in his discussion of נתן, see infra n. 275.

[104] E.g., Lev. 1:4, 3:2, 4:15, 24, 29, etc.

[105] This will be demonstrated in my forthcoming study on impurities.

[106] Similarly, see Exod. 29:33; Num. 28:22, 30, 29:5.

[107] Abarbanel, ad loc., perceives the sacrificial aspect of the Levites but he fails to follow through the implications of this insight. So does the *Kli Yaqar* (ad loc.) but he fuses it into the unproven and, in my opinion, unprovable thesis that the laying of hands upon the sacrificial animal involves the transfer of sin.

kippur money for the military census (Exod. 30:16; Num. 31:50; see 2 Sam. 24:1ff.)[108] and the *kippur* death for homicide (Num. 35:33; see 2 Sam. 21:1–16) and for idolatry (Num. 25:4, 11, 13; see Josh. 22:17f.; Ps. 106:29f.). All these cited cases share with Levitic *kippur* a common goal, stated explicitly in each case: to prevent God's wrath or plague (קצף/נגף)[109] from spending itself upon the entire community in addition to the sinners.[110]

The case of *kippur* money is more informative since it relates לכפר על נפשתיכם (Exod. 30:15, 16) and כפר נפשו (v. 12).[111] Thus the many-faceted root כפר is tied by context to its *qal* noun whose meaning is undisputed,[112] i.e., *kippur* money as

---

[108] The close relationship between the census and Midianite offerings is evident even in the description of their function. Both serve לכפר על הנפש and are placed לפני ה' for a זכרון on behalf of בני ישראל (Exod. 30:16 and Num. 31:50, 54).

[109] The term נגף/קצף is explicitly mentioned in connection with the census (Exod. 30:12, see 1 Chron. 27:24) and idolatry (Num. 25:9, 18f., 31:16; Josh. 22:17; Ps. 106:29) and alluded to in connection with homicide (2 Sam. 21:1, 3—blight); *kippur* incense has a similar purpose (Num. 17:11f.). Outside of P, see Exod. 32:35; 1 Sam. 4:17, 6:4; 2 Sam. 24:25; 1 Chron. 21:14, 22. These cases of *kippur* are not to be confused with *kippur* performed on the altar. The latter's purpose is to purge the sanctuary of its accumulated impurities lest they drive out the indwelling God (to be demonstrated separately); the *kippur* cases discussed here, however, have the immediate goal of preventing the already kindled wrath (קצף) from incinerating innocent and guilty alike.

[110] Having committed myself to the view that the two phrases (8:19 and 18:22f.) are parallel, I must, in all fairness, state the alternate possibility that they bear no relationship to each other and are, in fact, antithetical. Indeed, that one occurs at the inauguration of the Levitic office and the other where its role is redefined could encourage this alternate view. For then, the Levitic *kippur* would receive its explication by comparison with the impassioned action of Phineas at Baal Peor, also called a *kippur* for Israel (25:13*b*), and would mean that the Levite guard also stays God's wrath/plague when he cuts down the encroacher as Phineas cut down the apostate. This reading of Num. 8:19 would have the added virtue of now being a restatement of the two major Levitic functions: removal (עבדה, see §§ 52–64) and guarding (משמרת). As a result, the meaning of והם ישאו עונם and Num. 18 would remain unchanged, but the analogy with the Levitic ordination (Num. 8) would have to be abandoned.

However, this simple and, hence, attractive theory has built-in difficulties which outweigh its advantages. It would be the only place that assigns an active *kippur* role to Levites; it would break the *kippur* parallel with the Levitic sacrifices (supra) and, as a paraphrastic expansion of שמר משמרת, would be atypical of P's attested adherence to a set terminology.

[111] See Ehrlich, *Hamiqra Kifshuto* (1901) on Exod. 30:12, following Ibn Ezra on Lev. 1:1, 4. The etymological relation is difficult to prove; L. Moraldi, *Espiazione sacrificiali e riti espiatori nell' ambiente biblico e nell'Antico Testamento* (1956), pp. 220f., among others, doubts its existence. The question, to be sure, is not closed and merits reinvestigation. However, even if the investigation reveals that the text has indulged in folk etymology, the writer here—if not in all of P—believed the roots to be related. In other words, *kippur* as ransom is the supposition of the text. See also n. 114, infra.

[112] E.g., ‖ פדיון (Exod. 21:30). See also the homicide (Num. 35:31–33).

ransom.[113] Therefore, there exists the strong possibility that all the texts which construe *kippur* with קצף/נגף have *kōper* in mind:[114] innocent life spared by the ransom of the guilty parties or their representatives.[115]

§ 29. *Recapitulation*. Having posited that והם ישאו עונם implies Levitic culpability for lay encroachment, I have adduced a new verse (8:19) which parallels in structure and style the first text (18:22f.) whereby the phrase corresponding to והם ישאו עונם is לכפר על ב"י.[116] Moreover, if the discussion of כופר/כפר is valid, then the significance of the Levites' role in the sanctuary is now fully revealed. The Levites are ransom for Israel, a lightning rod to attract God's wrath upon themselves whenever an Israelite has trespassed upon the sancta. This, I contend, is both the consolation and the innovation in the answer to the

---

[113] All hail to Ibn Ezra (see Num. 8:19), the only one, to my knowledge, who saw the relationship. Moreover, the idea is not unknown to the ancient Near East, e.g., offering one's silver image as ransom to Shamash (*AMT* 90, i III, cited by E. Reiner, "La Magie babylonienne," *Le monde du sorcier* (Sources orientales 7, 1966) 85f. This notion is even more dominant in the Hittite religion, see M. Vieyra, "Le sorcier hittite," ibid., 110–115, 117f. For a convincing demonstration that Exod. 30:12–16 is of the earliest materials in P, dating not later than David, see J. Liver, "The Ransom of Half Shekel," *Kaufmann Jubilee Vol.* (1960) 54–67 (Heb.).

[114] Such a doctrine is not unknown to Wisdom, e.g., "The wicked is a ransom (כופר) for the righteous, and a renegade for the upright" (Prov. 21:18; see 11:8). Isaiah also speaks of a human *kōfer*: Israel's life is ransomed by the nations (43:3). Finally Phineas' *kippur*-execution for Israel (Num. 25:12) cannot be disassociated from his laudation: he "turned back My wrath from the Israelites," nor from the earlier demand for the public impalement of the ringleaders "so that the Lord's wrath may turn away from Israel" (ibid., v. 4). Here again we have a corresponding Wisdom teaching: "a king's wrath is a messenger of death but a wise man יכפרנה" (Prov. 16:14). Thus, both P and Wisdom counsel the removal of wrath by כופר/כפר. (So אכפרה פניו, Gen. 32:21, by extension. One is tempted to include the case of the Moabite crown prince, 2 Kings 3:27, as a tacit כופר/כפר, for its effect was precisely the same—if in reverse, since wrath was thereby shunted from Moab onto Israel.)
A footnote is no place to take sides in the raging controversy over the etymology of כפר (reduced, in the main, between the pan-Arabists' "to cover" and the pan-Assyriologists' "to wipe"). But that *an* aspect of the *pi'el* verb is related to the *qal* noun can no longer be gainsaid.

[115] It is also of moment that in rabbinic Hebrew the term "ransom" is expressed by a *pi'el* denominative, כפרה (so explicitly כופרא כפרה, B.Ḳ. 40*a*). In tannaitic literature, the word clearly stems from living folk vocabulary, used whenever the speaker wishes to take upon himself whatever evil might befall his fellow, e.g., M Sanh 2:1 (Tosef, ibid. 4:1); Tosef Shebu 1:4 (Yoma 1:12); M Neg 2:1. (An interesting example of how the original meaning is reversed in the passage of time is: "students of the Torah, who are the כפרה for the entire world, will not be affected by any of the demons," Tosef B.Ḳ. 7:6.) It is not that biblical כופר has changed into כפרה; כופר still survives in rabbinic Hebrew in the meaning of "fine." Is it perhaps that כפרה may be a verbal noun from the *pi'el* with the connotation "to ransom"?

[116] See supra n. 110 for an alternate view.

people's panic (Num. 17:28) in the wake of the plague (17:11–15). As table C (§ 23) makes clear, henceforth the Levites and priests are answerable for encroachment by the outsider (זר): priests for encroachment by fellow priests (18:7a); priests and Levites for encroachment by Levites upon the most sacred objects (18:3a, 5a); and Levites for encroachment upon the sacred enclosure by Israelites (18:3, 22, 23a). Only the last two are instances of vicarious culpability, but there is a difference between them: the guilty Levite imperils his fellow Levites as well as the priests; the guilty Israelite, however, dooms only Levites. The logic behind this distinction is evident. In each case, the guard who could have prevented the encroachment is blamed. An encroacher-priest (i.e., disqualified) need but penetrate the priestly guard to reach the most sacred objects: the encroacher-Levite must break away from his fellow Levites as well as through the priestly guards; the encroacher-layman commits his sin as soon as he penetrates the outer defense perimeter of the sanctuary which is manned by the Levites. Divine punishment, heretofore vented indiscriminately upon all of Israel, now befalls the responsible parties alone, the encroacher and the negligent Levites.

§ 30. *The new principle.* This last point implies an important caveat: the results are in nowise to be misconstrued as support for a theory of vicarious atonement/punishment in the Bible, i.e., that the innocent suffer for the sake of the wicked. To the contrary, my conclusions point the other way: innocent Israelites are ransomed by *guilty* Levites.[117] And if we find that all the Levites are held accountable for the negligence of a single Levite watchpost and all the priests and Levites for a single Levite encroacher, the principle which operates throughout is not vicariousness (i.e., substitution) but collectiveness.[118] Indeed, only from this perspective can we appreciate the dimensions of the innovation inaugurated by P. Whereas the doctrine of collective responsibility is a cornerstone of P's theology for all sins against God,[119] within the sanctuary there is an attempt to limit its destructive impact to the clergy alone. Herein lies the magnitude of the solace offered the panicky Israelites: henceforth, this cardinal

---

[117] Wisdom texts predicate this principle, supra n. 114. In other words, it is an orthodox Israelite doctrine.

[118] Collective responsibility, of course, is found in all the sources, e.g., the apostate city (Deut. 13:6), Achan's family (Josh. 7), Saul's sons (2 Sam. 21). However, as M. Greenberg has demonstrated ("Some Postulates," 5–28, esp. 20–28), biblical law predicates this doctrine only where the realm of the Deity is involved, but in criminal law individual culpability alone is the operating principle.

[119] Even though admonitions and precepts are directed to the individual, they are rationalized in terms of the collective; the fate of the nation is always inextricably involved, e.g., sexual immorality (Lev. 18:28; 20), the Sabbatical year (Lev. 26:34f.) idolatry (Num. 25:4, 9–13). If Josh. 22:20b means "And he, one man alone, did not die for his sin," then we have a deliberate attempt (perhaps in a P passage) to use the case of Achan as a means of underscoring the centrality of collective responsibility.

doctrine of collective responsibility shall be compromised for their sakes so that they may worship at the sanctuary without fear.

PERMISSIVE קרב/נגש

§ 31. *Definition.* That קרב אל can denote more than "approach"—the lexicons notwithstanding[120]—is borne out by a host of passages. We have already seen that where קרב is forbidden it means "encroach"; where permitted, it will now be shown, קרב אל means having legitimate access or becoming qualified, and should be rendered "have access to" or "be admitted to."[121]

§ 32. *Distribution.* The rules of קרב in the Korah pericope[122] are patient of both a positive and a negative rendering, as follows: "no outsider should presume (an outsider may not qualify) to offer incense" (Num. 17:5); the Levites "shall have no access to (may not encroach upon) the sacred vessels or the altar" (18:3); "an outsider shall not be associated with (shall not intrude upon) you" (18:4). Where there is no negation the permissive sense alone applies: "but you shall associate with yourself (הקרב אתך) your kinsmen the tribe of Levi" (18:2).[123]

Ezekiel is a particularly rich source of permissive קרב. Only after the priests change to street clothing, וקרבו אל "may they have access to the people" (42:14). Surely, since their official robes transmit holiness only upon direct contact,"[124] "approach" for קרב אל would be a gross distortion. Again we read: "they shall have access to My table to serve me" (44:16); since altar service obviously

---

[120] E.g., B-D-B, K-B, G-B. Among the translations, NJPS is a glorious exception. However, it is not always consistent, e.g., Num. 4:19; Lev. 22:3 (see infra n. 140).

[121] Of course, the basic meaning of "making contact" is also attested. For indisputable examples see Exod. 14:20; Ezek. 37:7, 17. The latter passages also suffice to refute Snijders' definition (p. 136) of קרב as "the coming into the proximity of another, viz. who is different . . . the gathering of what is unequal." Thereupon, Snijders explains Isaiah's use of הקריב (Isa. 5:8) that "the lands originally belonged to others and so do not belong together" (ad loc., n. 52). But what will he say of Ezekiel's use of the same root to express the rejoining of Israel's bones (Ezek. 37:7) and of the two sticks of Joseph and Judah "that they may be one" (v. 17)? See also n. 83 supra.

[122] See the comment on Num. 18:7, § 13.

[123] See also Exod. 28:1 where "bring near" for הקרב is meaningless.

[124] The priestly robes are categorized among the "most sacred" since they receive the oil of anointment (Exod. 29:21; Lev. 8:30). They might, therefore, fall under the ban of כל הנגע בהם יקדש (Exod. 30:29b). However, nowhere does P include the priestly clothing under this ruling. To the contrary, the fact that P applies the ban solely to the Tabernacle and its furnishings (vv. 26–28) and then lists the anointment of the priests separately (v. 30) leads to the conclusion that P emphatically disagrees with Ezekiel on this point.

requires contact, how misleading would "approach" be in this text![125] So, in all instances where the priest is the subject of קרב, access to and contact with sancta must be predicated—the very purpose for which the priesthood is established. Last, this positive sense of קרב is recorded even with the laity: the resident alien who wishes to offer the Pesach must undergo circumcision, ואז יקרב לעשתו "and then he shall qualify to offer it" (Exod. 12:48).[126] Again, "approach" for קרב would be patently absurd.[127]

§ 33. נגש. The analysis of קרב cannot be concluded without a comment on its synonym, נגש. A similar semantic range can be shown. A striking example is afforded by the Kohathites who "must not touch sancta, lest they die" (Num. 4:15);[128] priests dismantle the sanctuary ahead of them "so that they should

---

[125] The most frequent object of קרב is the Deity. This usage is original and literal rather than figurative and post-exilic, as claimed by Ehrlich, *Randglossen* (on Exod. 28:1), who hypothesizes a derivation from the terminology of the royal court, where the king's attendant is called קרוב (Esth. 1:14).

One example from the older Hittite world should suffice to nullify his theory: "Ihr 'Oberen' [ferner], die ihr der reinen [Pers]on des Königs nahekommt, seid auf (?) eure Reinheit bedacht (??) . . . und [je]ner kommt der Person des Königs nahe, (das) unter(liegt) dem Eid," "Instruktion für Prinzen, 'Herren' und 'Obere,'" §§ 26, 33–37, Einar von Schular, *Hethitische Dienstanweisungen* (1957) 28f. (but see A. Goetze's reconstruction of this text in *JCS* [1959] 13:65–70). See also Hittite Laws, §§ 187, 188, 199, 200A. Indeed, the prevalence of divine kingship in the ancient Near East assumes that the person of the king was treated as a god and similar taboos prevailed.

[126] For examples outside of P, see 1 Kings 2:7, 5:7.

[127] One is tempted to cite the many instances of קרב in statutes dealing with illicit sex where, obviously, more than "approach" is meant. So, for example ואקרב אליה‖ ובא אליה (Deut. 22:13f.; see Gen. 20:4; Isa. 8:3; and for P: e.g., Lev. 18:6, 14, 19, 20:16; Ezek. 18:6). This usage may have been deliberately coined as a euphemism, and is of no use to the etymologist. Moreover, euphemistic usage is attested in Akkadian from the time of Tukulti-Ninurta I (1242–1206). Another apparent euphemism in sexual matters is the use of ראה and גלה, usually with ערוה (for גלה in P, see Lev. 18:7–19, esp. v. 14, גלה‖קרב; for גלה‖ראה see Lev. 20:17, 17, 18; also Ezek. 16:37; Lam. 1:8). The root נגש is similarly used (Exod. 19:15).

Rabbinic tradition did not find the matter so obvious. For example, Maimonides (*Sefer Hamitzvot*, prohibition 53), on the basis of the *Sifra* Aharei 13:15 legislates that merely "approaching" is prohibited (see the *Megillat Esther* on the counter-argument of Nachmanides, ad loc.). Also, the euphemism theory cannot account for the choice of the "euphemisms": ראה, גלה, קרב. The strong possibility exists that *originally* the very exposure of and approach to the genitals were feared to be malefic. So indeed, most commentators explain the sin against Noah (Gen. 9:22[J]. For an exemplary discussion, see U. Cassuto, *A Commentary on the Book of Genesis*, part II, *From Noah to Abraham* [1964] 148–163, who implies that these verbs in Lev. chs. 18 and 20 should also be treated literally) and only at a later stage were these taboos treated figuratively.

[128] The verse implies that the sancta are covered, else the mere sight of them would be fatal (Num. 4:20). Furthermore, we note that though קרב/נגש and נגע both imply contact, they differ from each other by the principle of intention: whereas the

live and not die בגשתם אל the most sacred objects" (4:19). Since the Kohathites incur penalty only in touching the covered sancta but not in approaching them, בגשתם אל can only be translated "when they make contact with."

Similarly, Ezekiel will alternate the use of קרב and נגש whenever he has direct contact in mind: "The Levites shall not יגשו to Me to officiate as My priests ולגשת to all My sacred and most sacred objects. . . . Only the Levite-priests, the Zadokites . . . יקרבו to My table to serve Me" (Ezek. 44:13, 15f.). Since direct contact at the altar ("table") is required of the priest, the verbs must not be rendered "shall approach" but "shall have access." Moreover, since this Ezekiel passage with נגש is the precise equivalent of Numbers 18:3aβ, where קרב is used with the established meaning of access/encroach,[129] then נגש must also bear the same meaning.[130]

The verbs קרב/נגש are also found clustered in the texts dealing with disqualified priests. Again, the meaning of "have access" is verified. But this general meaning is patient of refinement into subtler hues which have important implications for the larger issue of sanctuary taboos. It is better, then, to treat the whole matter separately.[131]

§ 34. *Nuzi and the ancient Near East.* In view of the prevailing concept of the numinous in the ancient world, there can be no doubt that קרב/נגש in connection with sancta originally meant "approach." For the ancients, the numinous was an active force, extending beyond the physical boundaries of the sanctum so that its dangerous environs were also placed under taboo. A sampling of קרב equivalents from ancient Near Eastern texts should suffice to illustrate this point:

1. *Hittite:* "To the utensils (of thy worship) no one draws near."[132]
2. *Akkadian:* "An unclean person has come near the sacrifice."[133]

---

former is "encroachment" and implies a deliberate act, the latter may be accidental. And when the object of נגע is sancta, an accident must always be presumed (e.g., Exod. 29:37, 30:29; Lev. 6:11, 20).

[129] See The Composite, § 64 ad loc. and n. 76.

[130] On the basis of the logical axiom: things equal to the same thing are equal to each other.

[131] See §§ 37–39.

[132] "Daily Prayer of the King," *ANET*, 396f. See infra n. 206.

[133] CT 32:2, cited in *CAD*, s.v. *ellu*. See inter alia, R. Caplice, "Namburbi Texts in the British Museum," *Orientalia* (1967) 36:34, lines 1f.; E. Reiner, "Lipšur Litanies," *JNES* (1956) 15:137, line 85. B. Landsberger speaks of the afflicted's "circumambient danger" (cited in E. K. Ritter, "Magical-Expert and Physician," *Assyriological Studies* (1965) 16:302, n. 13). It is of special interest to note that the standard Mesopotamian idiom *muṛṣu lā ṭeḫû* also occurs in the Bible *in connection with disease:* ונגע לא יקרב באהליך (Ps. 91:10. See also Isa. 54:14 where מחתה, "terror," betrays the demonic provenience). In Israel, however, a transformation is evident; for there can be no doubt that קרב ב means direct contact (see Judg. 19:13).

3. *Egyptian:* "You may not come here, in the proximity of the sanctuary."[134]

4. *Greek:* "No one impure may approach (the sanctuary of Men at Sunion)."[135]

§ 35. *Nuzi qrb.* However, that the development from "approach" to "encroach" is not a peculiarity of biblical Hebrew but a natural linguistic phenomenon is attested by Nuzi Akkadian, and, strikingly, with the identical root *qrb.* The phrase *X ana ilāni la iqerreb*[136] is used "to guard against the possibility that the house gods may fall into unauthorized hands."[137] Thus, *qrb* in this context no longer means "to approach" but "to seize illegitimately" or "to encroach." Further confirming this meaning is that the verb *leqû* "to take" is used for the person who violates the prohibition of *la iqerreb.*[138] Thus, Akkadian reveals the same semantic development with *qrb* as attested in the Hebrew. It is also of no small significance that Nuzi is the original home of many peculiar terms found in Israel's customary and cultic law,[139] and it may very well be that the expanded usage of קרב was present in Israel's vocabulary from earliest times. In any event, there can no longer be any doubt that קרב meaning "encroach" is both contextually and linguistically certified.

§ 36. *Conclusions.* The transformation of *qrb* in biblical Hebrew, as I have shown, is thoroughgoing. Indeed, every single קרב/נגש has been reinterpreted to mean "encroach," *wherever penalties are stipulated.*[140] The philological history

---

Is there, however, not an equal likelihood that the Akkadian exhibits the same range? For example: *ana amēli teṭeḫḫi mimma lemnu lā iṭeḫḫīka* (cited by E. Ritter, ibid.), which must translate: "you may approach the afflicted without something evil affecting you," i.e., the second *ṭeḫû* may be figurative, as will be shown in the case of Nuzi *iqerreb,* below. Furthermore *ṭeḫû* and *qrb* are often used in synonymous parallelism with *snq,* "to press," when referring to the demoniac (e.g., Caplice, 36:4, line 11) and the meaning of direct contact would be assured.

[134] From the second gargoyle, east (E. IV 269, 4) cited in C. de Wit, "Les inscriptions des lions-gargouilles du temple d'Edfou," *Chronique d'Égypte* (1954) 57:29–45, p. 42. (See also E. IV, 112, lines 5f., 17f.; 286, line 11; 269, line 4; 275, line 10; 287, line 9).

[135] T. Wachter, *Reinheitsvorschriften im griechischen Kult* (1910) 7; also ibid., 71.

[136] JEN 89:10f.; 216, line 16. Hurrian *erwišše* is also used.

[137] Anne Draffkorn (Kilmer), *JBL* (1957) 76:216–224, esp. p. 221.

[138] E.g., Nuzi, Gadd, Kirkuk Tablets, no. 51, *RA,* 23, lines 14–21. Confirmation is now provided by Ras Shamra Akkadian, cf. J. Nougayrol, *Ugaritica V* (1968), text 2 (R.S. 17.21) line 11.

[139] E.g., בין טוב ובין רע, והחזקת בו, אשם, ערכך in E. A. Speiser's "Leviticus and the Critics," *Y. Kaufmann Jubilee Volume* (1960) 29–45.

[140] Another example, in addition to the citations above, is the case of the contaminated priest who makes contact with sacred food (Lev. 22:3). The language אשר יקרב... אל הקדשים... וטמאתו עליו corresponds almost word for word with the Akkadian citation, above. The biblical context, however, shows that קרב (here, too, attached to the death penalty, vv. 3b, 9) cannot mean literally "approach," for it would imply that a contaminated priest, unaware of his condition or of the presence of

of קרב/נגש, however, lies outside the scope of this study. Nonetheless, it is possible to state a tentative conclusion that קרב/נגש of the P source lies at the end of a long semantic development. The vocabulary of its contemporary and older non-Israelite analogues has been retained, but it has been filled with new content to meet the demands of the biblical faith. Moreover, as I have demonstrated, the specific reinterpretation of "encroach" is not Israel's innovation but is part of its linguistic heritage from Northern Mesopotamia.

Traces of the original "approach" still adhere to the "most sacred" objects, particularly the Ark, not only in the old narratives but in P itself, e.g., the mere sight of the sancta within the Tabernacle can be fatal for the unconsecrated. But these sancta, enshrined in the Temple and permanently out of view, are able to retain their ancient taboos, whereas the outer sancta, such as the altar and the sacrifices, in constant usage among the people, undergo the abrasions of historic change. The steady attrition noticed in the power of the impure is, therefore, accompanied by a reduction in the power of the holy, but not to the same degree. Specifically, the lethal range of a sanctum has shrunk from vicinity to touch and from chance to design.

This study of the cultic use of קרב/נגש demonstrates that its meaning goes beyond simple, physical approach to the more abstract amplifications "have access to," "be admitted to," "be associated with"; in prohibitions, as shown by the in situ contexts of הזר הקרב יומת, bolstered by Nuzi usage, it means "encroach."[141]

---

sacred food (even in his own home!—see v. 13) was guilty of a capital crime. אשר יקרב, then, is the idiom of encroachment and must be rendered "who deliberately handles" (not "partakes," NJPS). This pregnant verse, strictly speaking, is not eligible for analysis here; it belongs under the category of holiness-impurity contacts, to be treated separately.

[141] For the sake of completeness, it must be recorded that קרב and its equivalents are used by cultic prescriptions where literal "approach" is intended and where physical trespass is a violation. For some incontestable instances, note: Exod. 3:5; Lev. 9:8 (since slaughtering follows קרב); Josh. 3:4 (*ethnahta* under אליו; see Rashi). The *hif'il* הקרב אל provides a spate of examples. True, הקרב ל can mean to "present," "offer" where contact is involved (e.g., Lev. 3:9, 7:8) but not with the preposition אל, which always implies proximity. In fact all instances of הקרב אל have as their object either God (Num. 16:5, 9), the altar (Lev. 1:15, 2:8 [= Num. 5:25]; 6:7), the sanctuary entrance (Exod. 29:4, 40:2; Lev. 1:3) or the priest (Exod. 28:1; see supra n. 123; Lev. 2:8, see infra; 9:9 [a delicate point: Aaron may not take the bowl!])—and הקרב אל is purposely chosen in each case to express the notion of proximity.

Furthermore, we will never find the expression הקרב על (for 2 Kings 16:12, על > אל), i.e., הקרב cannot mean "to sacrifice" upon the altar. For על המזבח the verb is הקטר (e.g., Lev. 4:10; 1 Chron. 6:34; 2 Chron. 26:16) or העלה (more frequently outside P, e.g., Judg. 6:28); זרק/נתן (e.g., Lev. 22:22, but usually with blood); עשה (e.g., Exod. 29:38; Ezek. 43:27); הוקד (Lev. 6:6). Let us focus on the most frequent object, the altar. In each case where the preposition is אל, rather than ל, the altar's vicinity is deliberately intended. Thus, since the blood of the bird is of minute quantity, the officiating priest kills the bird at the altar so that its blood will drain immediately on

THE DISQUALIFIED PRIEST

There remains one final category of נגש/קרב prohibitions: the disqualified priest. It is predicated upon a basic distinction between the sanctity of the sanctuary and of the outer altar, a distinction as yet undisclosed.

§ 37. *The cases.* There are four disqualifications which prohibit priests from being in contact with the sanctuary and outer altar on pain of death:[142] improper washing, a physical blemish,[143] drunkenness,[144] and improper dress.[145] The texts follow in order:

בבאם אל אהל מועד ירחצו מים ולא ימותו או בגשתם אל המזבח לשרת להקטיר אשה לה׳

When they enter the Tent of Meeting they shall wash with water, that they may not die; or when they נגש the altar to serve, to turn into smoke an offering by fire to the Lord (Exod. 30:20; see 40:32).

אך אל הפרכת לא יבא ואל המזבח לא יגש כי מום בו

But he shall not enter to the veil[146] or נגש the altar, for he has a blemish (Lev. 21:23; see vv. 17, 18, 21, 21).

יין ושכר אל תשת אתה ובניך אתך בבאכם אל אהל מועד ולא תמותו

---

the altar wall (Lev. 1:15). Again, since only a "token" of the *minḥā* is burnt on the altar, the priest brings the *minḥā* up to the altar and then removes the "token" (Lev. 2:8 ‖ Num. 5:25f.; see Lev. 6:7). One text even uses לפני המזבח to leave it beyond question that the presented object will have no contact with the altar (Num. 7:10*b*). That the use of לפני is deliberate—to indicate proximity but not contact—is demonstrated by קרב in the *qal*, with man as its object and contaminated persons (Num. 9:6) or women (Josh. 17:4; see Num. 27:1f.) as its subject where, obviously, to keep one's distance is required by ritual or etiquette. Ehrlich, who notes this last point (on Num. 9:6), is confused by לפני ה׳. This phrase, however, is a synonym for פתח אהל מועד (see N. Raban, "The Entrance to the Tent of Meeting," *Tarbiz* (1951) 23:1–8, but with caution) and is irrelevant to our discussion.

[142] See § 2, table B2 and n. 18.

[143] Since the death penalty is not explicit for the blemished priest, the Tannaites deny its applicability; Rabbi Judah dissenting, derives it by analogy from Lev. 22:9 (Sifra, Emor 3:11). The rabbis of the Talmud, however, argue that the context of Lev. 22:9 is *sui generis*; see Sanh 83–84.

[144] Only the sanctuary is mentioned but the altar is implied (see Sifra, Shemini Par 1:4 and infra n. 147).

[145] The rabbis add a fifth disqualification: dishevelled coiffure (based on Ezek. 44:20 and Lev. 10:6; see Maimonides, *The Code: Sefer Avoda*, "Entrance to the Sanctuary," 1:8).

[146] The rendering "behind the veil" (NJPS, RSV; Noth, *Leviticus* ad loc.; Haran, "The Complex of Ritual Acts Performed inside the Tabernacle," *Scripta Hierosolymitana*, viii [1961] 272–302, esp. 274 n. 4) is surely wrong. This rendering would require the preposition מבית which is never synonymous with אל. אל, however, is the equivalent of את פני (Lev. 4:6, 17; see Rashi ad loc.). That the expression alludes to ritual acts before as well as behind the Veil, see infra n. 154.

Drink no wine or ale, you and your sons with you, when you enter the Tent of Meeting,[147] that you may not die (Lev. 10:9).

והיו על אהרן ובניו בבאם אל אהל מועד או בגשתם אל המזבח לשרת בקדש לא ישאו עון ומתו

They[148] shall be worn by Aaron and his sons when they enter the Tent of Meeting or when they נגש the altar to officiate in the sacred area[149] so that they do not incur guilt and die (Exod. 28:43; see 28:35).

§ 38. *The sanctuary.* The above verses state that the prohibition barring the disqualified priest from the sanctuary building is absolute; even if he has no intention to officiate, his entry is subject to death. This unconditional holiness of the sanctuary interior is emphasized by yet another prescription, the belled robe of the high priest: "Aaron shall wear it while officiating, so that the sound of it is heard when he comes into the sanctuary before the Lord and when he goes out—that he may not die" (Exod. 28:35). The wording of the text, that the belled robe is to be worn "when he goes out" as well as upon entry clearly indicates that it is the holiness of the interior itself rather than the cultic acts performed within that is responsible for this regulation.[150]

---

[147] The altar is missing in this prohibition but it must be supplied, as does the LXX. Rabbinic tradition derives it by analogy from the ritually unwashed, *Sifra* Shemini, Par 1:4.

[148] "They," strictly speaking, refers to the breeches. However, the verse concludes the pericope and, in the style of P, may sum up all the previous cases. Thus, all the priestly clothing may be included (see Lev. R 20:9; Tanḥ Aḥarei 6). Interestingly, the Talmud derives the death penalty for the lack of any of the priest's garments from Exod. 29:9aβ (Sanh 83b) and not from our verse. Is this a tacit admission that our verse (Exod. 28:43) speaks only of breeches?

[149] The rendering "sanctuary" is wrong, despite vv. 29 and 35, on the grounds of (1) grammar: the sanctuary, i.e., "the Tent of Meeting," has already been mentioned; (2) logic: the breeches are especially necessary when officiating on the outer altar (Lev. 6:3; see Exod. 20:26); hence, the object of לשרת "to officiate" must also include the altar; (3) meaning: קדש often means the sacred area (e.g., Lev. 10:17, 18 [note: בקדש]; 14:13; Ps. 63:3) and the same idiom, לשרת בקדש, elsewhere, can mean only "to officiate in the sacred area," e.g., Ezek. 44:27, "On the day he enters the sacred area (הקדש)—its inner court—to officiate in the sacred area (לשרת בקדש)," see n. 78 supra. Furthermore, since Aaron officiated at the outer altar only in his special vestments (בגדי השרד), it is probable that other usages of לשרת בקדש also refer to the sacred area, e.g., Exod. 35:19, 39:1, 41. That this plastic word can expand or contract to mean the inner shrine, the sanctuary or the sacred area, see M. Haran, "Priestly Image," 213, n. 17.

[150] So Nachmanides, ad loc., who cites two interesting reasons for the bells: (1) they ring "for permission (from the Deity) to enter"; (2) "that divine angels may not harm him." There can be no doubt, as students of comparative religion and folklore can attest, that this occult derivation is historically correct, except that in a monotheistic setting demonic powers are converted into agents of the one God. The Rashbam, followed by Ehrlich, explains the bells as a warning to other priests not to enter. Against this, however, is the incontestable fact that the high priest officiated inside

As established earlier, the deadly power of sancta within the sanctuary can be communicated to the non-priest on sight and not just by touch.[151] Now it is seen that the disqualified priest is considered a non-priest in regard to the sanctuary interior as long as his unfitness lasts. This holds true for all the temporarily disqualified: the ritually unwashed, undressed, and unsober. However, the blemished priest (Lev. 21:16–23) is treated differently. An explicit concession permits him to eat sacred food, even of the most sacred offerings (Lev. 21:22), just as later in the same text a concession is made for the impure priest to eat sacred food the evening following his ablutions.[152] Moreover, there is another change: instead of the expected formula, prohibiting the blemished priest from entering the sanctuary, we read: "But he shall not enter to the Veil" (v. 23a). This prohibition, I submit, also applies to the high priest, who alone may officiate within the sanctuary.[153]

The context confirms this observation. As the preceding unit has dealt with the high priest (vv. 10–15) we should expect the priestly disqualifications that follow (vv. 16–23) to include some reference to him. If, then, the verse refers to the high priest, why is a variation from the normal formula prohibiting sanctuary entry used? The answer is that "at the Veil" is the language of officiating;[154] the "Tent of Meeting" is the language of entry. Thus, the concession of sacred food to the blemished priest is supplemented by another concession: he may enter the sanctuary but (if he is a high priest) he may not officiate. Moreover, this concession is a logical deduction from the priestly system of scaled taboos: if the blemished priest is allowed direct contact with "most sacred" food he

---

alone only on the Day of Atonement (Lev. 16:27)—and he did not wear the bells (ibid., v. 4)! It is possible that he was alone when he purged the inner altar on other occasions (see Lev. 4:5–7, 16–18, 6:23), but most of his officiating, e.g., the daily ritual, surely did not find him alone. See also Haran, *Scripta*, 286–288, 294f., n. 26, for additional discussion.

[151] See table B6, § 33, and nn. 22, 128. For the opposing rabbinic view see n. 162.

[152] "For it is his food" (v. 7b) is the language of concession. The priest, in this instance, is treated no differently than a layman who had contracted a minor impurity (e.g., Lev. 15:16f.). Originally, it seems, the contaminated priest was subject to severer restrictions.

[153] See Haran, *Scripta*, 274–285.

[154] That Lev. 21:23 refers to the high priest was correctly noted by Ibn Izra followed by Abarbanel, ad loc. Their intuition is confirmed by the correspondence of the idiom אל הפרכת with the total ritual of the high priest, daily at the Menorah and inner altar (Exod. 30:7f.), weekly at the Table (Lev. 24:5–9), and in severe cases of impurity, at the altar and before the Veil. All the inner sancta stand close to the Veil; the altar, "before the Veil" (Exod. 30:6); the Menorah, "outside the Veil" (Exod. 27:21; Lev. 24:3); the Table, "outside the Veil" (Exod. 26:35). לפני means "directly in front" or "center," applicable only to the altar. Also, the use of the purification blood is expressly "before" (את פני). The Bechor Shor also sees in this verse a reference to the high priest, but to his *kippur* ritual, see n. 158. In any case, entrance behind the Veil is naturally excluded by both the expression and the taboos involved.

surely cannot be denied contact with any other "most sacred" object,[155] i.e., the sancta of the sanctuary. Thus we see that priestly disqualifications are not all of equal severity, and that physical blemishes, in particular, are less exacting than the other three disqualifications.[156] Perhaps the later rabbinic controversy on whether a disqualified priest is unconditionally prohibited from the sanctuary or whether he is only prohibited from performing the ritual[157] is a reflex of the biblical distinction between blemishes and other priestly disqualifications. In this controversy, the distinctions between the sanctuary and the outer altar may also play a part, which I turn to now.

§ 39. *The altar.* The prohibitions in regard to the outer altar involve us again with קרב/נגש. However, in contradistinction to the sanctuary prohibitions which are absolute, those of the altar are qualified, as follows: (1) for the ritually unwashed, "to serve, to turn into smoke an offering by fire to the Lord" (Exod. 30:20); (2) for the physically maimed, "to offer the food of his God" (Lev. 21:17; see v. 21);[158] and (3) for the ritually undressed, "to officiate in the sacred area" (Exod. 28:43).[159] Clearly, קרב/נגש is, in each case, an auxiliary to a main verb having to do with officiating at the altar, and therefore must be translated

---

[155] Excluding the inner sanctum which, though most sacred, is of higher rank.

[156] There are two plausible reasons for the leniency: (1) The blemish is permanent (despite *Sifra,* Emor, Par 3:5; M Bek 7:1). Even if temporary, it is of longer duration than the others and cannot be ended at will. In the meanwhile what is the priest to eat? (2) Other disqualifications are deliberate acts. Here an accident of birth or mishap is implied. In other words, the principle of intention is invoked (for another area of the holy where intention operates, see supra n. 128). Perhaps, then, the absence of the death penalty for the trespassing blemished priest is not by chance. So indeed, the Sages rule versus R Judah (Sanh 83a [ber.]; see 84a; Maimonides, *Code: Seder Avoda,* "Entry to sanctuary" 6:2 who prescribe flagellation instead) though they admit, initially, that the blemished priest is even forbidden to enter the courtyard area between the altar and the sanctuary (M Kel 1:9; *Sifre Zuta* on Num. 5:2, and see the following note).

[157] The language of M Kel 1:9 and *Sifre Zuta* (on Num. 5:2) implies absolute prohibition, as affirmed categorically by the *Megillat Esther* (see *Sefer ha-Mitzvot* of Maimonides, Prohibition 73): "Every (mention of prohibited) entry (into the sanctuary) includes entry for any purpose whatsoever, whether for officiating or not." On the other side of the argument, see Nachmanides on Maimonides, *Sefer ha-Mitzvot,* Prohibition 73 (see 69) and his commentary on Lev. 10:7, and R Samson of Sens on M Kel 1:9. Interestingly enough, at least one temple in Ptolmaic Egypt sided with the former—the absolute prohibition; see H. Junker, "Vorschriften für den Tempelkult in Philä," *Analecta Biblica* (1959) 12:151–160, esp. II, lines 10f.

[158] These verses (17 and 21) cannot but refer to the altar. I have refrained from citing v. 23, though the altar is mentioned, since no ritual is included. Indeed, it is possible with the Bechor Shor to understand that the inner altar is intended. Thus, all of v. 23 would refer to the high priest's ritual of *kippur* within the sanctuary, which consisted of two parts; the sprinkling of blood before the Veil and the daubing of blood on the inner altar; see n. 154, supra.

[159] See n. 149.

"to be admitted," "to have access," precisely as in the other cultic passages investigated earlier.[160] The disqualified priest who violates the altar prohibition is not one who approaches or even touches it, but one who encroaches, who attempts to officiate upon it.[161]

§ 40. *The distinctions.* Thus, we must conclude that the inner sancta and outer altar do not stand on the same level on the scale of holiness, even though both are called "most sacred" (Exod. 30:26–29). The disqualified priest (except the blemished) may not enter the sanctuary but he may contact the altar, i.e., his sanctity is suspended with respect to officiating at the altar but not to touching it.

This distinction between sanctuary and altar also obtains in other matters. For example, the non-priest is prohibited from viewing the inner sancta but is only forbidden to touch the altar (in the open courtyard and visible to all).[162] Also, the composition of the sancta bespeaks this sanctity differential: the sanctuary objects are plated with gold, the altar with copper; in transit, the former are covered with a blue cloth, the latter with a purple cloth.[163] Since it is now clear that the sanctity of the altar does not reach that of the sanctuary, it is only natural to expect that the altar taboos will not be as severe. And so it is. The distinction already observed for the non-priest (seeing the inner sancta and

---

[160] See § 33.

[161] Josephus writes that "surrounding both the sanctuary and the altar was a low stone parapet, fair and graceful, about a cubit high which separated the laity from the priests" (*Wars* V, 5:6–7). One tannaitic text, while not speaking of a physical partition, sets off the space of four cubits around the altar as an area of higher sanctity, into which disqualified priests had no access (*Sifre Zuta* on Num. 5:2; the four cubits also figure in Tosef Yoma 1:12, and see M Yoma 2:1). If so, then קרב/נגש may have been interpreted literally as "approach" in later second Temple days. However, see H. Albeck's demurrer on Josephus' parapet (note on M Mid 2:6), attributing it to Alexander Jannaeus (*Ant.* XIII, 13:5) and hence irrelevant to our discussion.

[162] Rabbinic tradition, it must be added, denies categorically that either Levites *or Israelites* incur any penalty in touching the most sacred objects with the exception of the Ark (for the Levites, see *Sifre Zuta* on Num. 18:3; for Israelites, see *Sifra* on Lev. 6:2); only encroaching is forbidden, supra 55. As for Num. 4:20, where sight of the inner sancta is expressly prohibited, Rabbi Judah, in the name of Rab, interprets כבלע as referring to the dismantling process, but not when the sancta are stationary (Yoma 54a).

[163] The LXX and Sam. add (Num. 4:14) that the washbasin and its stand were also covered with purple cloth. Note also: "Because the altar of the whole-offering was not inside it was not covered with blue but purple" (Num. R 4:17), i.e., the Rabbis recognized that the altar is of lesser sanctity because it is farther removed from the center of holiness. According to Haran, "Priestly Image," 201, blue cloth is more expensive. These two distinctions between the altar and sanctuary in regard to their composition were recognized by Haran, ibid., 206f. (for an ostensible third, see infra n. 165), but the crucial subject of the disqualified priest was unfortunately overlooked.

touching the altar) is now matched by a distinction for the disqualified priest:[164] he is barred from contact with (even sight of) the sanctuary sancta but not with the altar.[165]

§ 41. *Recapitulation.* All disqualified priests are enjoined from officiating but have full use of the sanctuary courtyard, including contact with the outer altar. Access to the sanctuary, however, is strictly forbidden, except to the blemished priest who is permitted contact with most sacred objects, be they food or sancta. Also, קרב/נגש prove to be auxiliaries to verbs denoting officiation at the altar, and must be rendered "be admitted" or "have access," as in the passages dealing with the outsider (זר) and others. The disqualified priest and outsider are not completely identical in this respect since the former may have contact with the altar and the latter may not.[166]

---

[164] Except the blemished, see n. 156.

[165] Haran, *Scripta*, 280–282, 298–299, argues for another distinction between sanctuary and altar, that the high priest wears his special vestments only while officiating inside the Tabernacle but not at the altar. His reasons, which follow, are not compelling: (1) The vestments are too costly, magnificent, and unwieldy for such bronze altar tasks as "splashing blood, cutting up carcasses, washing entrails, etc." However, the latter two acts are done by other priests; and in private offerings, by the laity (so explicitly, Lev. 1). The former act is performed with utmost care (see M Zeb 5:3; *Sifra*, Vayikra Ned Par 4:9f., etc.). (2) The High Priest of the second Temple officiating at the altar is "a secondary interpretation of the word of the Mosaic Law." On the contrary, it is good witness for biblical practice (see Lev. 16:24). (3) Haran admits that this distinction is nowhere stated but adds that P is silent about many assumptions. We have shown to the contrary that the biblical source for the use of the high priest's vestments (Exod. 28:43) explicitly mentions the altar (see also my exegesis of לשרת בקדש, n. 149).

[166] The earliest rabbinic sources are uniformly insistent that the Tabernacle courtyard comprised two different grades of holiness: the area between the entrance and the altar, corresponding to the פתח אהל מועד (see § 12) and the rest of the courtyard, which they refer to as בין האולם ולמזבח between altar and tent (e.g., M Kel 1:9; *Sifre Zuta* on Num. 5:2, ed. Horovitz, p. 228). The main distinction, according to the Sages, between this inner section of the courtyard and its two neighboring areas is that disqualified priests could have access to the outer courtyard section but not to the inner (though R Meir, the apparent opponent to R Yosi in the Mishna [see Tosef Kel B.Ḳ. 1:6: also comp. Tosef Suk 4:23] does not apply this prohibition to the improperly washed priest), and that the qualified priests could idle in the inner section but could only enter the sanctuary if they officiated there (Tosef ibid.).

The name בין האולם ולמזבח is biblical (Joel 2:17), but its status is not; for the Bible contains not a single law, not even a hint as to its special sanctity. Yet the unanimity of the tanaaitic sources—reflecting, therefore, historic reality at the end of the second Temple—forces us to believe that this dual division of the court of the priests goes back to older, indeed biblical, times.

According to Y. Aharoni, "Arad: Its Inscriptions and Temple," *BA* (1968) 31:2–32, the courtyard of the newly excavated Israelite temple at Arad (strata XI and X: Solomonic and ?) "was divided by a step (a remnant of the ancient altar) into outer

THE SINAITIC PRECEDENT

§ 42. *Nachmanides.* Finally, I turn to an account which has great bearing upon this injunction—the theophany at Sinai (Exod. 19). True, it lies outside of P,[167] but it is certainly essential to it or rather, preliminary to it, for it heads up all the textual material attributed to the year-long stay at Sinai (Exod. 19:1– Num. 10:10) in which P predominates. The astute comment of Nachmanides[168] merits being relayed in full:

> Hereafter the Tabernacle in the Wilderness is zoned as Mount Sinai was zoned, since the Divine Glory was also thereon. And He commands: "the outsider הקרב shall be put to death" (Num. 1:51) as He said there: "for he shall surely be stoned" (Exod. 19:13); and He commands "let not (the Kohathites) go inside and witness the dismantling of the sanctuary" (Num. 4:20) as He warned there: "lest they break through to the Lord to gaze" (Exod. 19:21); and He commands: "you shall guard over the sanctuary and the altar" (Num. 18:5) as He said there: "The priests also, who come near the Lord, must purify themselves . . . let not the priests or the people break through to come up to the Lord" (Exod. 19:22, 24).

§ 43. *Other parallels.* Nachmanides' parallels are striking but they do not exhaust the comparison. For P, Mount Sinai is the archetype of the Tabernacle, and is similarly divided into three gradations of holiness. Its summit is the Holy

---

and inner parts" (p. 22). Aharoni goes on to conjecture that "the inner part, about one third of the total, may be equated to the biblical *ulam*" (ibid.). This identification, I am convinced, is without foundation, chiefly because (1) the *ulam* of Solomon's temple was enclosed, (2) the two stone bases standing before the Arad *hekal*—probably holding the equivalent Jachin and Boaz pillars—are *within* the purported *ulam* whereas in Solomon's Temple they probably stand in the open, *before* the *ulam*, and (3) the *ulam* is strictly an appendage of the *hekal*, as reflected in the rabbinic tradition: it has no special sanctity of its own. (Indeed the Arad sanctuary, without an *ulam*, resembles more the Tabernacle than the Temple.)

A far more plausible suggestion, I submit, is that the Arad courtyard is divided according to its late second Temple counterpart. Thus, not only are all the above objections met, but a puzzling archaeological feature of the Arad sanctuary is explained. As the floor plans clearly indicate (ibid., figs. 12, 15, and 16), the dividing step projects from the altar itself, from the side facing the *hekal*. It is a graphic and literal fulfillment of the terminology, coined to indicate the boundaries of this inner section: בין האולם ולמזבח. If I am correct, the Arad sanctuary has provided archaeological evidence for the subdivision of the court of the priests in first Temple days.

[167] The source attribution is in dispute. For O. Eissfeldt (*The Old Testament: An Introduction* [1965] 191–194) it is the most ancient Pentateuchal source. For more standard analyses, see M. Noth, *Exodus, OTL* (1962) 153–160; S. R. Driver, *Exodus* (1911) ad loc. Nevertheless, the fact that the introduction to the Sinai pericope (19:1, 2a) is clearly the hand of P means that the Priestly source incorporated the older account and let it stand at the head of his description of the Tabernacle and its cult. See further n. 170.

[168] See his introduction to the book of Numbers, also on Exod. 25.

of Holies;[169] God's voice issues forth from there (Exod. 19:20) as from the inner shrine (Exod. 25:22; Num. 7:89); the mountaintop is off limits to priest and layman alike (Exod. 19:24b) and its very sight is punishable by death (Exod. 19:21b), and so with its Tabernacle counterpart (cf. Lev. 16:2 and Num. 4:20); finally, Moses alone is privileged to ascend to the top (Exod. 19:20b; see 34:2b) just as later, the high priest is permitted entry to the inner shrine under special safeguards (Lev. 16:2ff.).

The second division of Sinai is the equivalent of the outer shrine, marked off from the rest of the mountain by being enveloped in a cloud (Exod. 20:21, 24:15bff.[P]; see 19:9, 16) just as the cloud overspreads the entirety of P's Tabernacle (Num. 9:15ff.).[170] However, the entire mountain is not covered. Moses is able to ascend some distance with the priests and elders (24:1) and separately with Joshua (24:13) until the cloud perimeter, at which he probably leaves Joshua (see 32:17) when God calls him to enter the cloud. Thus, below the cloud is the third division, called "the bottom of the mountain" (19:17, 24:4), a technical term for the lowest portion of the mountain.[171] Here is where the altar and stelae are erected (24:4). It is equivalent to the courtyard, the sacred enclosure of the Tabernacle to which priests alone have access except for the forecourt "entrance" where the layman brings his sacrifice, provided he is in a pure state.[172] Here too is where the people witness the theophanies of the

---

[169] Sinai's top is ablaze (24:17); its equivalent is the pillar of fire that was seen over the Tabernacle. Both fires, moreover, were enveloped in a cloud; see infra.

[170] When the camp is on the march, however, the cloud rises and is suspended over the dismantled Tabernacle parts (Num. 9:15ff. [P]). JE's concept of the shrine, as is well known, calls for the cloud to lead the Israelites in march (Exod. 13:21f.) and to descend only for oracular purposes, and in front of the Tent, not over it (Exod. 33:9f.; Num. 12:5). How does Moses know that God wishes to speak with him, according to P? In my opinion, the sign is given by the cloud-encased fire (God's כבוד, see Exod. 24:17) which is normally visible only at night (Exod. 40:38), but now becomes so luminous it can be seen in daylight (Num. 20:6; see Lev. 9:23f. and esp. 2 Chron. 7:3). When the firecloud descends upon the Tabernacle (Exod. 40:34) or leaves it (Ezek. 10:4a), it expands into the courtyard (ibid., 4b) so that the consecrated personnel cannot enter (Exod. 40:35; see also 1 Kings 8:11; 2 Chron. 7:2), i.e., the power of the numinous is increased in motion.

What is significant here, and startling, is that Sinai's concept of God's firecloud resting above the mountain-shrine corresponds with P and not JE, just as the mountain itself, in its threefold gradation of holiness, is also P's sanctuary and not JE's. What this means for source criticism cannot be entered into here. A reappraisal, however, is certainly indicated; see also n. 167.

[171] Obviously, there is no exact point at which the plain stops and the mountain begins. Where the incline is clearly distinguishable marks "the bottom of the mountain."

[172] The point near the cloud perimeter to which the elders and priests ascend for a closer view of the deity (Exod. 24:10) might correspond to the area between the altar and the Tabernacle entrance which, though not of "most sacred" character, is the exclusive reserve of the priests (see supra n. 166). That lay elders including Joshua

Tabernacle and Temple at their respective consecrations (Lev. 9:4f., 24 and 2 Chron. 7:3). Similarly, at Sinai: the nation is first purified (19:10f., 14f.) and then brought out of the camp to the viewing stand at the foot of the mountain.

Thus the blazing summit, the cloud-covered slopes and visible bottom rim correspond to Tabernacle divisions, and the analogous tripartite holiness of Mount Sinai and the Tabernacle is confirmed.

Of immediate relevance for this study is the Sinaitic injunction כל הנגע בהר מות יומת "whoever touches the mountain must be put to death" (19:12b).[173] Its parallel construction to our formula is obvious. The similarity is all the more striking because of יומת, for these two are the only violations against the sanctuary or its sancta that call for death by man (§ 2, table A). The reason can be only their common rationale: to prevent divine wrath from venting itself not just upon the intruder but upon the people at large. True, the telltale term נגף/קצף does not appear at Sinai but its presence is nonetheless felt, e.g., "lest He break out against them . . . and many of them perish" (19:22b, 24b f., 21b). P, however, cannot turn to Levite guards to siphon off the wrath, for the rebellion of Korah has yet to be born.

ORIGINS

§ 44. *Clues.* Can a date be assigned to the origin of the formula? Since it is ensconced within undatable cultic provisions, it seems pointless even to ask. Yet I would suggest that a chronological framework, however vague, can be deduced from the very wording of the formula, without recourse to its contexts. Indeed, that it occurs four times in precisely the same form and that each time

---

accompany the priests is no problem for P since it calls for the consecration of the priesthood only after the Tabernacle is erected (Lev. 8; cf. Exod. 28f.). That is why we read that both laymen *and* priests require the express order of God to allow them even the short distance beyond the people's stand (24:1). The mention of priests is probably an anachronism; the suggestion that they stand for the first-born is untenable, since we have no evidence that the first-born served as priests (see Ehrlich, *Randglossen*, ad loc.). To the contrary, the sacrifices at Sinai are offered neither by priests nor by first-born but by "young men," most likely chosen on the spot (24:5).

[173] The use of נגע instead of קרב is most instructive; it proves once again that קרב in relation to sancta cannot mean literally "approach." For why should Sinai whose holiness is surely greater than most sancta (e.g., the outer altar) be prohibited from touch, whereas the lesser sancta be prohibited from "approach"? קרב must, therefore, be lower on the scale of holiness than נגע; and our definition of "encroachment" fits perfectly here.

Moreover, the use of נגע further corroborates our picture of Sinai as the Tabernacle archetype. לא תגע בו is the precise equivalent of אל אהל המועד לא יבא; i.e., touching Sinai corresponds with entering the Tent. The principle of intention plays no part here as with קרב (§ 16); even accidental contact is fatal.

it is awkward to its context[174] indicates the likelihood that the formula had its own independent history.

First, I realize that a terminus a quo is not within reach. Fear of illicit contact with the holy informs man's earliest societies. The further back we go the more we read of divine wrath devastating a whole community for the sin of a few. It is, therefore, understandable that trained guards should be posted about a sacred area to ward off intruders.

The next clue is יומת, and the conclusion to which it led, that the Levite guards are armed to kill. Later tradition could indulge in the fancy that the sanctuary cordon played an honorific role befitting the dignity and grandeur of the King of Kings.[175] However, Israel's God was as in need of burly bodyguards as any royal monarch. This is the ineluctable, if paradoxical, concomitant of Israel's monotheism and severs it from its pagan forbears and contemporaries. As long as the world of demons was alive, the gods needed divine defenders—counter forces from the same superhuman realm—to keep watch over the sanctuary.[176] But with supernal evil eliminated and malefic action concentrated solely in human hands, the sanctuary needed to be protected only against man, and for this task human guards were sufficient.

How far back can we trace Levite guardianship over the Tabernacle? The evidence is sparse and ambiguous. True, we have the Chronicler's unintentional admission—the most authentic kind—that he knows of Levite guards in his own day.[177] He, furthermore, relies upon the tradition of P that the guarding and removal of the Tabernacle are two main Levite functions which—he adds on his own—continued in force up to David's time. On the other hand, we hear nothing of Levite guards in the Temple in the book of Kings; Jehoiada uses

---

[174] I do not wish to imply that the formula is a later insertion, but only that when the codifier wanted to convey this law he resorted to a formula already at hand rather than compose one in his own style. For example, the singular of this formula stands out in startling relief against its plural-voiced contexts. Moreover, in Num. 3:38, having concluded with בני ישראל, the text does not continue with the same subject or a pronoun (or a purpose clause, e.g., 18:22), but uses a synonym, והזר, and in the singular! Clearly, a previously coined formula is being used.

[175] *Sifre Zuta* on Num. 18:4 (ed. Horovitz) 292; *Yalqut Shimoni*, § 752 (end).

[176] Examples from *ANET* should suffice: *Egyptian*—The Repulsing of the Dragon and the Creation, 6f., The Repulsing of the Dragon, 12; The God and His Unknown Name of Power, 12–14; Curses and Threats, 327 (section b). *Hittite*—Ritual for the Purification of God and Man, 346; Evocatio, 351–353. *Mesopotamian*—The New Years Ritual, 331–334, esp. lines 381f.; Temple Kettle-Drum, 334–338, lines 14–16; Enuma Elish, 60–72: I, lines 61–64; IV, lines 61f., 91; VII, lines 32f.

[177] See our discussion, § 7. That other Levite professions such as Temple musicians probably have pre-exilic antecedents, see W. F. Albright, *Archaeology and the Religion of Israel* (1942) 125–129; W. Rudolph, *Chronikbücher HAT* (1955) 91 (followed by J. M. Meyers, *Chronicles I* (1965) on 1 Chron. 9:26b–32) and J. S. Licht, "Levi," *Ency. Miq.*, IV, cols. 467–472, esp. 470f. (Heb.).

soldiers not Levites to watch over Joash in the Temple.[178] Still, if P's historical memory is correct,[179] then we have to turn to the early traces of the Levites for the probable roots of their guardianship over the sanctuary.

§ 45. *Levi the Tribe.* Indeed, P's concept of Levite guards accords best with the picture of the Levites in the oldest narratives of Genesis and Exodus. We find them a secular tribe not a sacral class, and they have a belligerent, trigger-happy record. Their sacking of Shechem (Gen. 34; 49:5–7) is accepted as reflecting historic fact.[180] Their slaughter of their fellow Israelites in the Wilderness (Exod. 32:25–29) is in keeping with their military prowess and temperament, and their demonstrated loyalty to Yahwe may anticipate or reflect their later role in the sanctuary.[181]

§ 46. *The Priests and Phineas.* Another clue to the antiquity of the Levite sanctuary guards is the repeated insistence of the P source that the priests had a share in this role. I have already noted that the formula, in three out of the four occurrences, is addressed to the priestly guard (Num. 3:10, 38, 18:7) and that the security of the sancta is entrusted exclusively to the priesthood. Furthermore, P does more than give idealized cultic ordinances; it supplies a concrete, historic example—Phineas at Baal Peor (Num. 25:1–15). True, the guarding of sancta by priests is nowhere mentioned in this passage. However, the basic data point in this direction: (1) *the person:* Phineas' father is Eleazar, "in charge of

---

[178] There are priests called שמרי הסף "threshold guardians" (e.g., 2 Kings 12:10, 22:4, 23:4, 25:18; compare their Hittite counterpart, § 49) who are called Levites by the Chronicler (1 Chron. 9:19, 22; 2 Chron. 23:4, 34:9). Since the word for "threshold" is also found in the plural in passages relating to the Temple (e.g., Isa. 6:4; Amos 9:1) it is not certain whether the thresholds of the gates to the Temple court or the entrance to the Temple is meant. In any event, P's supposition of Priestly guards within the main entrance and around the sancta (see supra n. 33) is corroborated as early as the Hittite cult (see § 48) and by Hellenistic and tannaitic evidence of late second Temple practice (see n. 34). Therefore the observation that the Levites are absent from Kings still stands.

[179] It is in so many other institutions it describes, e.g., tithes; see Y. Kaufmann, *Toledot ha-Ernuna ha-Yisralit*, 4 vols. (1938–1956) *The Religion of Israel*, abridg.-trans. by M. Greenberg (1960) 189–193. (An early provenience for its materials not for its composition is herewith being argued, see §§ 50, 75.)

[180] See R. de Vaux, *Ancient Israel* (1961) 368.

[181] The Blessing of Moses (Deut. 33:9) may contain a reflex of this event. Other critics feel that the verse describes a characteristic and not an event (note the general wording of v. 9b), and is rather a tribute to Levi's impartiality in justice (so S. R. Driver, *Deuteronomy*, ICC [following Onkelos]; see 400f. for his references). A third and preferable interpretation, I would suggest, sees in this verse a reference to function: the on-going task of carrying the Ark (Deut. 10:8) and the other sancta. If so, the supposition of a pre-monarchic date for the poem would be strengthened. See F. M. Cross and D. N. Freedman, "The Blessing of Moses," *JBL* (Sept. 1948), 67:191–210, for other reasons. For the latest literature, see Eissfeldt, *The Old Testament*, 227–229.

those guarding over the sacred objects" (Num. 3:32);[182] (2) *the place:* at the entrance to the sanctuary (v. 6*b*);[183] (3) *the act:* "he took a pike in his hand, etc." (v. 7*b*); (4) *the result:* "and the plague was checked" (v. 8*b*). Thus, the son of and successor to the chief[184] of guards strikes down a leading culprit from Israel and Midian and thereby stops the plague. The text also implies that had the ringleaders been slain earlier (v. 4*a*), many of those who died in the plague (v. 9) could have been saved (v. 4*b*). In brief, even though the incident deals with apostasy rather than encroachment upon sancta, we are given a vivid image of Phineas' "impassioned act for his God" (v. 13); it describes the ideal behavior of the sanctuary guard.[185]

§ 47. *The final clue: shared custody.* According to P, priests and Levites are sharply distinguished from each other in all their functions: the priests alone may officiate at sacral rites; the Levites, however, may only assist in the preparations. The Levites, in turn, have a monopoly over the porterage of the sacred cult objects;[186] the priests have no share in this honor. Both sacerdotal classes, however, share the custody of the Tabernacle, priests within the sacred area and

---

[182] שמיר משמרת הקדש is also used for the definition of the Kohathite guarding duties during the march. הקדש, therefore, must refer to the sancta which the Kohathites carried.

[183] For the enigmatic קבה, see de Vaux, *Ancient Israel*, 297, for its possible connection with the pre-Islamic *qubba* and for a bibliography on the subject.

[184] He is called chief (נגיד) of the guards by the Chronicler (1 Chron. 9:20).

[185] Since the act may have taken place within the sacred enclosure (vv. 6*b*, 8*a*), actual encroachment may be involved. For the Levites in a similar role, see Exod. 32:27–29 and see § 62 on the *qubba* and the antiquity of P's Ark; P converges on JE on this point.

[186] M. Haran, *Ency. Miq.* IV (1962), s.v. Priesthood, col. 24 (Heb.), maintains that P does not allow the Ark to leave the Tabernacle in accordance with later Temple practice (1 Kings 8:8) though all sources admit it was mobile before (Deut. 10:8, 31:9; Josh. 6:6, 12; 1 Sam. 4:4–6; 1 Kings 2:26, 8:3–6). However, this prohibition is nowhere stated in P. P's silence can hide the existence of ceremonial norms (e.g., we have no details on the daily incense ritual) but it is hard to accept that P would consciously omit a prohibition, particularly one dealing with Israel's most sacrosanct cult object. To the contrary, it is much more plausible to assume that P agrees with all the early sources that the Ark was taken into battle but does not concern itself with the Holy Wars except in regard to the ritual purity of the soldiers (Num. 31:19–24) and to set up a standard formula for the allocation of spoil to the sanctuary and its personnel (ibid. 25–54). Indeed, one verse (ibid. 6) explicitly tells us that trumpets were taken by Phineas into the battle together with the כלי הקדש. These can neither be the priestly vestments (G. B. Gray, ad loc.) nor the Urim and Tummim (TJ followed by NJPS), for כלי הקדש in P is generic for part or all of the sancta (e.g., Num. 3:31, 4:15, 18:3). P is therefore telling us that appropriate cult objects accompanied Phineas into the fray, and the Ark may have been one of them. (The trumpets, not being anointed, were technically not כלי קדש and therefore, had to be listed separately.)

Levites without.[187] Moreover, twice we are told that Levites can be summoned by the priests to assist them in guarding inside the sacred area (Num. 3:7a; 18:3a) provided they do not encroach upon the sancta (18:3b, 5a).

What should be made of this guarding function of the Levites, shared with the priests and yet so minutely differentiated from them? Gray writes in his commentary, echoing the prevailing Wellhausenian point of view:[188] "The existence of a Levitic caste, separate and distinct from the priestly, was unknown to the Mosaic age, unknown even to the age of Josiah: it belongs alike in theory and practice to the post-exilic age." Subsequent scholarship differs little from his conclusions, except perhaps on the question of "theory," which many now claim was developed in the Josianic period.[189]

In my opinion, an ab initio conclusion should point in the opposite direction. That the custody of the sanctuary is shared by priests and Levites harks back to the earliest period of Israel's history when Levite-priest distinctions were yet fluid and contested (e.g., Korah)—since all Levites were eligible to serve as priests—and when the entire tribe of Levi had as its primary cultic role to guard the Tabernacle and its sancta (see further § 62). On these antecedents the Bible itself is silent, but a significant extra-biblical source brings aid:

§ 48. *The Hittite "Instruction for Temple Officials."* Pertinent lines will be quoted in full and followed by comment:[190]

a. *Two classes of guards*

On the outside beat[191] keepers[192] shall watch; inside the temples shall the temple officials patrol all night through and they shall not sleep.[193] (III, 9; see 26–30)

---

[187] So M. Noth, *Exodus* (on Exod. 32), 245, 250f.; see supra n. 33. The tradition that both priests and Levites perform guarding functions continued to the last days of the Temple; for tannaitic references see n. 34.

[188] *Numbers*, 24.

[189] R. de Vaux, *Ancient Israel*, 362ff.

[190] There are two extant translations: E. H. Sturtevant and G. Bechtel, *A Hittite Crestomathy* (1935) 149–174 (hereafter referred to as HC) and A. Goetze, "Instructions for Temple Officials," *ANET* (2nd ed., 1955) 207–210. Being a non-Hittitologist who cannot decide between conflicting translations, I have thought it best to cite both versions where the differences are critical for the meaning of the text. I am deeply grateful to the eminent Hittitologist, Professor H. G. Güterbock, for generously answering my numerous queries concerning the meaning of the original Hittite. The following notes (191–205) are based on information provided by him.

[191] "Outside the enclosure" (*ANET*). "Outside the precinct" (*HC*). In either case, *araḫza ḫali* has a spatial sense, see infra nn. 203 and 209.

[192] *LÚḫaliyattalla* is the technical word for "watchman" (see also III, 22, 23, 29f.), assigned to a *ḫali*, see below, n. 203. The translation "keeper" is adopted from *HC* in order to distinguish him from the guards inside the temple area. See nn. 194 and 209.

[193] *ANET* (except as noted above).

At once, we notice that there is a clear-cut distinction between the guards [194] within the temple and those outside. This distinction is rigorously maintained throughout the text. Moreover, it can be shown that the temple officials are priests [195] whereas the keepers are non-priests. Biblical priests and Levites show a similar differentiation: both have guard duty in the sacred area, the priest on the inside and the Levite on the outside (Num. 3:7, 18:3).

b. *The guards at the gate*
Furthermore, someone of those who are priests shall be in charge of the gate of the temple and guard the temple. (III, 13f.)[196]

The entrance to the Hittite temple is guarded by a priest and not a keeper. So in Israel; though the Tabernacle area is surrounded by a Levite cordon, the entrance to it is guarded by the priests (Num. 3:38, 18:2*b*).[197]

c. *The head of all the guards*
Night by night one of the high priests shall be in charge of the patrols. (III, 12)[198]

The Levite clans are also under high priestly control: The Merarites and Gershonites under Ithamar (Num. 4:28, 33) and the Kohathites under Eleazar (Num. 4:16).[199] The latter, the high priest designate (Num. 20:26–28), is chief of all the Levite guards (Num. 3:32).

---

[194] The technical word for guards is *LÚwehiškattalleš* (III, 7, 12) from *wehešk*, lit., "continually turn about," hence "patrol" (so *HC*), "walk the beat." Two kinds of guards are distinguished: the *haliyattalleš* ("keepers") who patrol on the outside and the LÚ.MEŠ.É.DINGIR.LIM ("temple officials") who patrol within. See the next note.

[195] The temple officials are mentioned in I, 48; II, 36, 59, 64, 80; III, 3, 10, 28; and IV, 78. From III, 3, "whoever (is) a temple official—great priests, small priests, and all IM.ME-priests" (*HC*), it is apparent that the term "temple official" can be used as a generic for the Hittite priesthood. This meaning is confirmed by the colophon (IV, 78): "The first tablet of the duties of all the temple officials, of the kitchen workers of the gods, of the farmers of the gods, and of the cowherds of the god, (and) the shepherds of the god, is finished." The listing here corresponds with the order of the officials addressed in the text. But the paragraphs dealing with the menial servants (headed by "kitchen workers") are preceded by instructions to various orders of priests, all addressed by name. It is therefore clear that in the colophon they are subsumed under "temple officials."

[196] *ANET.*

[197] That the שמרי הסף of the first Temple were priests is not only explicitly stated (2 Kings 12:10) but is to be inferred from the priestly company they keep (2 Kings 25:18 ‖ Jer. 52:24) and from their access to the היכל (2 Kings 23:4). Chronicles, to be sure, calls them Levites (1 Chron. 9:19; 2 Chron. 34:9). This, however, is another instance of the conflict between Chronicles and P (e.g., 1 Chron. 9:19*b* versus Num. 3:29), and probably reflects the practice of the second Temple of the Chronicler's day (versus Licht, col. 469).

[198] *ANET.*

[199] The biblical assumption is that Aaron is too old to engage in the strenuous duties of his office, and these are assigned to his sons.

d. *The keepers assist the temple officials inside*

If a keeper is assigned to anyone he may also enter the enclosure. He must not speak thus: "I am guarding the house of my god but I will not go in there." If there is some talk of enmity, (namely), that someone will undertake to defile Hattusa and (the keepers) at the outer wall do not recognize him, but the temple officials recognize him inside, the keeper shall definitely go after him. (In) such (situation the) keeper must not fail to spend the night with his god. (III, 23–30)[200]

According to Hittite cultic law, the keeper must leave his station outside the temple area to perform guard duty within if so commanded by the temple officials. Two cases are cited: escorting the layman who comes to the temple for a sacred rite and searching for or guarding against the unauthorized who may have slipped into the temple area.

According to P, the Levite will also leave his post to escort the lay worshipper into the sacred area, at "the entrance of the Tent of Meeting," to assist him in his sacrificial preparations (Num. 16:9) and to assist the priest in protecting the sancta against encroachment (Num. 3:6b, 7a, 18:2–4). In these prescriptions we also find the same insistence that the Levite must perform these duties inside the sacred area at the bidding of the priests.[201]

e. הזר הקרב יומת *and the responsibility of the guards*

But if it is [a foreigner], if it is not a Hittite man, and he ap[proach]es the gods, he shall be killed. And he who conducts him (into the temple), it makes him liable of the death penalty too. (II, 9–11)[202] Furthermore, let the watch[203] be divided among you; then the one in whose watch sin occurs shall die; let him not be pardoned. (III, 18–20)[204]

---

[200] *ANET*.

[201] These texts leave no doubt that the Levites are subservient to the priests. From the outset: "place them in attendance upon Aaron the priest to serve him" (Num. 3:6); עמד לפני is the language of subordination (see 1 Sam. 16:22; 1 Kings 1:2). Ch. 18 underscores this theme by the idiomatic use of את = under, e.g., ובית אביך אתך "your fathers' house (i.e., the Kohathites) under your charge" (v. 1); הקרב אתך (instead of אליך) "qualify . . . under your charge" (v. 2). וילוו עליך (instead of עמך) "and be attached to you" (v. 2) is also an expression of subordination, as noted by Ehrlich, *Randglossen*, ad loc.

[202] *ANET*.

[203] *ḫali* is the technical term for "watch," "nightwatch." In the latter case it is one of the three vigils into which the Hittite night was divided, analogous to Akk. *maṣṣartu* A. Goetze, "On the Hittite Words for 'Year' and the Seasons and for 'Night' and 'Day'," *Language* (1951) 27:467–476, esp. 473, n. 20, and adopted by J. Friedrich, *Hethitisches Wörterbuch* (1952) s.v. *ḫali*. This term is also patient of a spatial as well as a temporal meaning: "beat" (H. G. Güterbock, "Wachbezirk," *JCS* (1952) 6:35f. with special reference to our text); "enclosure," "precinct" (*ANET*), see n. 192. Since a guard is assigned both an hour and a beat, "watch" could encompass both the temporal and spatial meaning.

[204] *HC*, except "watch" for "precinct." *ANET* reads "(Responsibility for) the precinct shall be divided among yourselves. He who commits an offense with respect to the precinct shall be killed. . . ."

The biblical formula can be spotted in the first line in clear view. There is the outsider, the זר, who in the Hittite world is the foreigner; [205] his crime is קרב, "he approaches [206] the gods" by being unlawfully inside the temple area; his punishment is יומת, death by man. Moreover, whoever conducts him into the temple is also put to death; this may refer to the elite layman permitted access to the temple (II, 6f.) or the keeper performing escort duty (III, 26f.; see d, supra). Finally, the temple official in whose beat a sin occurs is punished by death. In sum, any offense within the Hittite temple area is a capital crime for the offender, for his escort (if he has one), and for the temple official on guard duty.

The above, I suggest, represents two widespread norms in the ancient Near East. Elsewhere we also find that unauthorized trespass into the temple area is punishable by death. The Hittite text supplies a second norm: the mortal guilt of the guard on watch. Here, a biblical analogy comes to mind. Jehu stations his guards around the Baal temple in Samaria and warns them, "The man who allows any of those whom I give into your hands to escape shall forfeit his life" (2 Kings 10:24*b*).[207] The Hebrew reads נפשו תחת נפשו. This "life for life" or "man for man" policy was then the norm in critical military situations.[208] It is surely not far afield to suggest that it was always in effect in the residence of the god, the critical source of the community's weal.

§ 49. *Recapitulation.* The Hittite "Instructions for Temple Officials" give a series of regulations for the guarding of a temple in pre-Israelite times against which we can measure the corresponding provisions of the Priestly Code. First and foremost, we see that the Hittite cult, anterior to the Bible, differentiates between two classes of temple guards which correspond to the biblical priests

---

[205] *araḫzenaš*, "foreigner," is mostly restored but even without it we have "not a man of Hattuša," i.e., a non-Hittite. There is also a class of foreigner ᴸᵁ*UBĀRU* (Akk.), a dignitary, perhaps a member of the diplomatic corps who was admitted into the Hittite temple (II, 6). For a discussion of this term see E. von Schuler, "Hethitische Kultbräuche in dem Brief eines ugaritischen Gesandten," *RHA* (1963) 72:45f. (I am indebted to Professor Harry A. Hoffner for this reference.)

It has been claimed that the exclusion of foreigners qua foreigners from Israel's Temple is unique in the ancient world (see E. J. Bickerman, "The Warning Inscriptions of Herod's Temple," *JQR* (1946–1947), 37:387–405, esp. 390); the problem must now be examined anew.

[206] The text, if properly restored, reads *t*[*i-ya*]-*zi*, and means "stand," analogous to Akk. *nazāzu* (Friedrich, *Wörterbuch*, s.v.). The Hittitologist R. Stefannini adds, in a private communication, it "is a very generic verb of intransitive movement" and he points to its use in the Hittite Laws, 187, 188, 199, 200A (*HL, HG*, and *LI* versus *ANET*) and esp. in the "Daily Prayer of the King," XXIV, 1:2 (*ANET*, p. 397); see also supra § 34. Though not literally "approach" it would imply, I believe, "to be in the presence of," a fair approximation. In any event, the Hittite text evidences the pre-biblical stage of our formula when קרב meant physical proximity.

[207] The case of Jehu is military; the factor of the temple is purely accidental.

[208] The mortal culpability of a watchman is also reflected in Ezekiel's parable (33:1–9). Cf. also 1 Kings 20:39, 42 and Ehrlich, *Randglossen*, ad loc.

and Levites not only in generic outline but in sharp detail. For the Hittite "Levite" is also under command of a high priest, is stationed outside the sacred area,[209] escorts the layman requesting a rite into the sacred area, pursues or guards against an intruder into the sacred area[210] at the command of the priests, and suffers death if he is responsible for unlawful trespass. The Hittite priest, as his Israelite counterpart, guards the temple, its sacred court and its entrance,[211] and pays with his life for any sin which takes place on his watch.

§ 50. *The antiquity of the formula.* Whence P's concept of the shared custody of the Tabernacle? That we find it in the second Temple from the Chronicler's day on (§ 7 and n. 34) is surely due to the canonization of the

---

[209] The construction of the Hittite temple differs in a basic way from the Tabernacle in that the sacred court where the laity assemble for worship is at or near the center of the Temple so that the worshippers have to be admitted into the Temple in order to enter the court (similar to Cretan and Babylonian temples). The shrine is one of the rooms on the outer wall of the Temple, at times jutting beyond it so that the statue of the god can be illumined through side windows facing the outside. (See the floor plans of five Hittite temples in K. Krause, "Boğasköy Tempel V," *Istanbuler Forschungen*, XI [1940] pl. 6, partially reproduced in O. R. Gurney's *The Hittites* [1952] 146, fig. 9. The plan of the entire complex of the largest of these temples is drawn in H. Frankfort, *The Art and Architecture of the Ancient Orient* [1954] 119, fig. 47.) Since the sacred court is within the Temple proper, it is clear that the Temple officials do guard duty within the court too.

In Israel's Tabernacle, the balances are reversed: the sanctuary is within the courtyard and not the other way around. Yet, the basic distinction notwithstanding, the division of guarding duties is precisely the same: the priests and not the Levites are responsible for the courtyard.

[210] An obvious difference should not be overlooked. Whereas the biblical Levite and layman had no access into the Temple (and its adjoining portion of the court), their Hittite counterparts faced no such restrictions. Indeed, even a class of foreigners was admitted into the temple itself, see supra n. 205.

[211] Haran, "The Priestly Image," 223–226 detects a contradiction in P: whereas the layman is given access to a portion of the sacred enclosure between the entrance and the altar, "P's system betrays an implicit tendency to regard the whole enclosure as the exclusive domain of the priests." As evidence of the latter he cites: (1) The very existence of a curtained enclosure "any contraction of which would constitute a violation of approaching the holy objects." (2) "The priests encamp and help 'guard' in front of the enclosure's gate." (3) "The enclosure screen is of the very same weave as the outer veil of the Tabernacle," i.e., of equal sanctity.

To answer his points seriatim: (1) There are many prohibitions in P against contact with the Tabernacle and outer altar; but there is not even one that prohibits the layman's entry to the enclosure (except when he is impure, e.g., Lev. 12:4). This is no accident but follows inexorably from P's own system. For the enclosure is not "most sacred" as are the Tabernacle and altar but belongs to the lower category of the "sacred." A simple proof of the inferior holiness of the court is evidenced by the Day of Atonement ritual (Lev. 16). Just "most sacred" areas are purged: the shrine, the sanctuary, and the outer altar, but not one drop of purgatorial blood is sprinkled upon the enclosure floor or curtains. The latter, not being "most sacred" does not receive the *kippur* rite. (One will also recall that on the day of consecration, the enclosure alone was not anointed, see Exod. 30:26–30, 40:9–16.) According to P, however, only the "most

Pentateuch. That it is not evidenced in the first Temple throughout its entire existence is attested both by the silence of Kings (especially the implied contradiction in Joash's rebellion, see §§ 7, 44) and by the direct testimony of Ezekiel (nn. 41, 47). Clearly then, it could not have been mediated via the Canaanites. For, if it was not a feature of the first Temple (though Solomon had no compunctions about borrowing freely from Canaanite–Syro–Hittite* models), how could it be a product of a subsequent generation which would hardly have dared to invent a new tradition of temple guarding, not to speak of supplanting the first Temple practice with a patently pagan imitation? Thus, there is every reason to suspect that P's tradition stemmed from Israel's own past. The existence of a similar pattern in the second millennium Hittite society now converts suspicion into conclusion.

---

sacred" is off limits to the layman, but no harm ensues from his contact with "the sacred." Thus Haran's contention of P's "implicit tendency" to concede all of the enclosure to the priests is not only wrong but is the opposite of the fact. For in P's system, the layman theoretically has access to the entire enclosure. True, the inner portion of the enclosure between the altar and the Tabernacle was regarded by the priests as their exclusive reserve (for which we may even have archaeological evidence, see supra n. 166), but this distinction is not recognized by P or any other Pentateuchal source. This is why some later rabbinic sources could argue on behalf of lay access to the inner court. (On the processions around the altar on the Feast of Tabernacles see M Suk 4:5 and Albeck's note p. 476; also idem on M Mid 2:6. Is perhaps Ps 26:6 a confirmation?)

(2) The priestly guard at the enclosure entrance and (3) the latter's special veil only highlight the importance of the entrance as over against the rest of the enclosure. In pagan temples, entrances and thresholds were also guarded and purged more than other parts. Here is where the gods had to pass when they were taken out in procession. Here is where images of protector gods were erected. Above all, here is where apotropaic rituals were performed: purgations, fumigations, and incantations to protect against incursions of demons (see n. 176). Greater vulnerability leads to greater taboo, and the reflex is still observable in Israel (e.g., Ezek. 45:19). Haran to the contrary, the selection of the entrance for greater sanctity is itself proof that the rest of the enclosure is of lesser sanctity!

Finally, our Hittite text should clear up any remaining doubts on this matter. The Hittite "priests" also guard in the court and at the entrance (see n. 209 for the structural variation) and yet the "Levites" who normally guard outside are expected to conduct the laity into the sacred area and even to lodge there at the behest of the "priests" (note Num. 18:2, 4a). Thus for Israel and the Hittites, the sacred enclosure may have been under the priestly control, but the non-priest had his rights too.

In the final analysis, Haran is really constrained to set the entire enclosure outside of the lay sphere because of his literal interpretation of קרב as "approach." However, no sooner is it rendered "encroach" all difficulties vanish. Now the layman may approach the Levite and Priestly cordon about the sacred area and at its entrance; he may even approach the sancta exposed in the forecourt (but not the Tabernacle) or carried in transit. He approaches as far as the sacred guards will allow. After this warning, his "approach" turns to "encroach," and הזר הקרב יומת.

* See now D. Ussishkin, "Building IV in Hamath and the Temples of Solomon and Tell Tayanat" *IEJ* (1966) 16:104–110.

One caveat must enter at this juncture. These Hittite parallels do not prove the antiquity of the priests and the Levites, per se; they only demonstrate the antiquity of one of their sacred functions; the guarding of the sanctuary. But the gain is nonetheless substantive. It means that as long as Israel had a sanctuary at all, the likelihood exists that there were two classes of sanctuary guards; if not priests and Levites then proto-priests and proto-Levites. In any event, one is no longer left to wonder why P has sharply distinguished priests and Levites from each other in every function except the common duty of guarding the sanctuary. The latter represents a tradition that reaches back to the earliest tribal memories of a guarded cultic shrine. Indeed, the Tabernacle as a wilderness tradition begins to assume literal reality.

It should also no longer be surprising that P demands the life of both the negligent guard (Levite or priest) and the offender. The inference purely from the biblical evidence that the sanctuary guard is commanded to kill all trespassers else his own life is forfeit is now fully corroborated by at least one anterior text in the world of the Bible. This alone, apart from the literary and historical evidence adduced, is sufficient to warrant the antiquity of the formula.

הזר הקרב יומת is thus seen as an authentic artifact from the earliest levels of Israel's history. That it has survived is due both to the tenacious hold characteristic of cult formulas, in general, and to the specific plasticity of the term קרב which could be reinterpreted from original "approach" to "encroach" and thus enable the entire formula to be molded by the demands of Israel's monotheistic faith.

§ 51. *The contrasts.* Two major differences between P and the Hittites are projected into bold relief by our formula, and since they tell us much concerning the postulates of biblical religion a special word on them is in order.

1. In Israel, the delinquent guard is punished by the Deity and not by man (see nn. 26 and 76). This change from ancient Near Eastern norms cannot be haphazard but is the result of a consciously formulated and methodically applied principle which operates throughout the Priestly Code. It is that sins against God are punishable only by God.[212] This is a second confirmation[213]—in addi-

---

[212] The episode of Gideon merits special attention: "Will you contend for Baal? Or will you defend his cause? Whoever contends for him shall be put to death this morning. If he is a god, let him contend for himself, because his altar has been pulled down" (Judges 6:31, RSV, except reading עד = עוד with Y. Kaufmann, *Judges* [1962] ad loc. [Heb.]; see Job 1:18; Neh. 7:3). It is a concise paradigm of the biblical polemic against idolatry and its universal regulation, now confirmed by our Hittite text, that crimes against the Deity are punishable by man. Moreover, if my understanding of this verse is correct, might it not be that the editor intends that Joash's challenge be flung not merely against his townsmen but against all of heathendom and, thus, this legal premise of P activates other biblical sources as well?

[213] The study of כרת, to be published separately, will provide a third confirmation.

tion to the study of יִמֻּת/יוּמַת (tables A and B, § 2)—of what can now be clearly
seen as a basic postulate of Israelite cultic law, that one's offense to the Deity is a
private affair except when it jeopardizes the immediate welfare of the community.[214] Death of man is juridically valid only when human life has been or
will be lost, in avenging bloodshed or in preventing bloodshed. Thus the encroacher must be struck down by the guards lest divine wrath vent itself upon
the guards themselves (originally, the populace; see §§ 15–24). The death sentence
upon the delinquent guard (and his fellows), on the other hand, can await the
long arm of heaven since his crime is solely against the Deity and does not
imperil the rest of the community.

2. In P, all the guards share the culpability of the negligent guard (for the
hierarchy of responsibility, see table C, § 23); in the Hittite cult, however, the
principle of "man for man" operates. In my opinion, this difference is imaginary;
a due contrast exists but in a different dimension altogether. The opening
exhortation in the "Instructions for Temple Officials" illustrates it tellingly:

> Are the minds of men and of the gods generally different? No! With regard to the
> matter which we are dealing? No! Their minds are exactly alike. . . . And if a
> slave causes his master's anger, they will either kill him or they will injure him at
> his nose, his eyes (or) his ears; or [they will seize] him, his wife, his children, his
> mother, his sister, his in-laws, his kin whether it be a male slave or a slave-girl.
> They may (either) *impose the extreme penalty*, (or) they may do to him nothing at
> all. If ever he is to die, he will not die alone; his kin will accompany him.
>
> If, then, on the other hand, anyone arouses the anger of a god, does the god
> take revenge on him alone? Does he not take revenge on his wife, his children, his
> descendants, his kin, his slaves, and slave-girls, his cattle (and) sheep together
> with his crop and will utterly destroy him? Be very reverent indeed to the word of
> a god! (I, 21–38)[215]

---

[214] We have already seen that no cultic crime, i.e., committed against the Tabernacle or its sancta, is punishable by man, and that the execution of the encroacher is
not a legal punishment but an act of self-defense on the part of the Levite guards, § 24
(and of his Hittite counterpart too, § 44). Table A, § 2, has also shown us that there are
only a handful of religious crimes which call for death by man, and these are all explicable in terms of their disruptive impact upon the society. Certainly abusing parents and
incest are crimes that fall under the jurisdiction of the family patriarch and his life and
death powers in these matters are never questioned. The Sabbath violator and the
medium, if unpunished, contribute to the breakdown of the religious discipline and
morale of the entire community. Though idolators should also fall under the death
penalty for the same reason (as in Deut. 13:16, 17:5), their death is not prescribed by P
with the exception of the Molech worshipper, but his death may be due to filicide and
not to idolatry. The three remaining cases have their individual raison d'être: the
blasphemer has contaminated all within earshot and only his immediate destruction
(preceded by "hand laying") can remove the impurity; the proscribed person is an
authorized human sacrifice; and ascending Mount Sinai falls into the same category
as the קרב and is indeed its archetype, see §§ 42f.

[215] See *ANET*.

It should be abundantly clear from this text alone (see also III, 44–54) that corporate guilt is very much alive in Hittite law. That it is restricted to one's family and slaves does not set it apart from P, since priests and Levites are conceived as blood brothers, members of a single family-tribe.[216] To the contrary, it is the similarity of Hittite and Israelite conceptions which is striking since in both divine anger consumes the offender and his family. Thus, for the Hittites a "man for man" principle operates when the temple offender is slain by man, but when his death is dealt by the gods his family shares his fate.[217] In Israel it is no different. P itself provides two paradigms—the Molech worshipper (Lev. (20:1–5): if the community does not put the offender to death, then God will punish him and his family (v. 5); and the case of Korah, Dathan, and Abiram (Num. 16:23ff.): "and the earth opened its mouth and swallowed them up with their households . . . and all their possessions" (v. 32).[218] Thus, it is clear that divine punishment of a household is a norm in P and, indeed, in all biblical sources,[219] and the transfer of punishment from the nation of the offender to his tribe, instanced by the errant Levite guard, is entirely in keeping with established biblical and contemporary norms.

Nonetheless, a contrast exists. The Hittite case of the household of the slave sharing the latter's punishment does not have its counterpart in the Bible. As demonstrated conclusively by M. Greenberg,[220] Israel's criminal law has rejected the doctrine of corporate culpability; "this was exclusively the way of God; it was unlawful arrogation for man to exercise this divine prerogative."[221] Thus the principle of individual culpability, operative in Hittite law for the punishment of the delinquent guard, is abruptly altered to corporate culpability

---

[216] In the locus classicus for Levitic responsibility (Num. 18:1–6) it is no accident that the brotherhood relationship is emphasized. Note בית אביך (v. 1 and cf. 4:18); אחיכם (v. 2); אחיך (v. 6).

[217] Our text: I, 30–33; II, 74; IV, 52f., 74. Even the death penalty imposed upon the families of delinquent slaves by the king ("Instructions for Palace Personnel to Insure the King's Purity," *ANET*, 207) can be explained as the action of the deity, since the offenders have all taken an oath of loyalty to the king in the god's name every month, and in cases where their disloyalty is only suspected, they must undergo an ordeal, i.e., the god himself designates their guilt.

[218] The text is in some confusion since we learn later that the sons of Korah survived. For a recent treatment see J. Liver, "Korah, Dathan and Abiram," *Scripta Hierosolymitana*, VIII (1961) 189–217. For another possible interpretation of the Molech sin, see Greenberg, "Some Postulates," 28.

[219] E.g., Achan (Josh. 7); Jabesh Gilead (Judg. 21:10f.); Saul's sons (2 Sam. 21); and in theory: Exod. 20:5 (Deut. 5:9); Deut. 13:16. These instances, however, are not of one hue and must be carefully distinguished, see Greenberg, "Crimes," 736*b*.

[220] "Some Postulates," 20ff.

[221] Ibid., p. 27. Greenberg also cites this last quotation from our Hittite text (*HC*'s version, found in Gurney, 70f.).

in dealing with the inferior delinquent slave.[222] In Israel, on the other hand, corporate culpability remains a theological doctrine but is never allowed to leave the celestial sphere to control the jurisprudence of man.

---

[222] We have already hedged this generalization in n. 217, supra. Another Hittite text, "The Proclamation of Telipinus," *HC*, 183–193, gives us further pause. Its main purpose is to prevent the doctrine of corporate culpability from operating within the royal household, else the sin of one of its members can result in the elimination of the entire royal line. Yet the fact that such a proclamation had to be issued is proof that the principle was operative in Hittite society. And even if the proclamation was followed, it applied only to the family of the king. The general prohibition of Deut. 24:16, actually enforced by King Amaziah against his father's murderers (2 Kings 14:6), is beyond the Hittite horizon.

III. THE TERM עבדה

§ 52. *The error.* The substantive עבדה and its verb עבד occur some forty and twenty times, respectively, in connection with the duties of the Levites. Modern dictionaries and translations invariably render them as "service" and "to serve."[223] This translation, I submit, is at best misleading and, where Levitic עבדה is involved, totally wrong. The Levites of the Priestly source do not officiate at rites; they do not even assist in them. Moreover, the Tabernacle, the outer altar, and their respective utensils are forbidden to them on pain of death (Num. 18:3).[224] Only when the Tabernacle is in transit may the sacred objects be handled by one Levitic clan, and then only after they have been covered by the priests (Num. 4:15ff.).

§ 53. *Definitions.* We have already seen that P invests the Levites with the responsibility of משמרת (guard duty) over the Tabernacle both in camp and on the march;[225] עבדה introduces us to their second major responsibility: moving the Tabernacle.[226] However, this term betrays other nuances which must be meticulously defined.

---

[223] So "service at the Tabernacle, *Gottesdienst* (cultic) service," K-B; "service (of God)," B-D-B; Dienst, G-B (partially qualified in no. 3).

[224] For details, see § 23.

[225] See §§ 4–8.

[226] There is a third: "to minister to the community to serve them" (Num. 16:9). Ibn Ezra, alone among the exegetes, correctly identifies this function as the assistance rendered by the Levites to the Israelites in the preparation of their sacrifices. The layman must pass through a Levitic watchpost in bringing his sacrifice to "the entrance of the Tent of Meeting" (see § 12). It then becomes the responsibility of the Levites to keep him under guard lest he encroach upon sancta (see further §§ 9–15 and the Hittite analogue, § 49). It is only natural to expect that his Levitic "escort" will also provide him assistance with the non-cultic, preparatory acts, e.g., slaughtering, flaying, washing, which normally are performed by the layman (cf. Lev. 1:5, 6, 9). This prescription to provide aid to the worshipper, given in vague form and only here in the Pentateuch, becomes of major magnitude in undisputably post-exilic texts. It is clearly the peg upon which Ezekiel fastens his demand that the responsibility for ritual slaughter be transferred from laymen to Levites (Ezek. 44:11, 46:24; see also § 73). According to the Chronicler, Levites were co-opted for flaying (2 Chron. 29:34, 35:11) as well as slaughtering (2 Chron. 30:17), but, as these cited verses indicate, only under emergency conditions. For the larger importance of Num. 16:9 see The Composite, n. 272.

I shall demonstrate that Levitic עבדה never veers from its root meaning of "physical labor," and that within that range it can refer to (1) physical labor, in general; (2) the job of moving the Tabernacle, in particular; and (3) a portion of this job, either (a) to dismantle and reassemble the Tabernacle or (b) to transport it. It is possible to determine which meaning of עבדה the text has in mind by looking for a description of the job in each context. For example, if עבדה means the job of dismantling and reassembling the Tabernacle (definition 3a), it is because for the Levites in question only this aspect of Tabernacle removal involves their physical labor.

§ 54. *General removal.* That עבדה means basically "physical labor" (definition 1) requires no verification. Turning instead to the second usage of Levitic עבדה, moving the Tabernacle, the locus classicus is Numbers 8:25f.: "At the age of fifty they shall be discharged מצבא העבדה (from the work force) ולא יעבד עוד (and shall labor no more). They shall assist their brothers לשמר משמרת (in keeping guard over) the Tent of Meeting ועבדה לא יעבד (but they shall perform no labor)." Here עבדה cannot refer to the Levites' general duties for it is sharply distinguished from their responsibility for משמרת. עבדה must have specific meaning. It is clear that it requires physical exertion, otherwise retirement would not be set at age fifty. That the starting age for עבדה is set for thirty (other texts give twenty-five or twenty),[227] is further indication that its conscription age corresponds to the span of man's maximum physical power. As the textual loci of עבדה, adduced below, will demonstrate, there can be no doubt that עבדה must refer to the job assigned the Levites to move the Tabernacle and its appurtenances during Israel's wanderings in the Wilderness.[228] The Tabernacle's prefabricated, mobile parts must be dismantled, transported, and reassembled from station to station.

§ 55. *The components.* The three components of Tabernacle removal are expressly stated in the first passage on the work of the Levites: "They shall transport (ישאו) the Tabernacle and all its furnishings . . . the Levites shall take it down (יורידו) . . . the Levites shall set it up (יקימו)" (Num. 1:50f.). In Numbers, chapters 3 and 4, where the term עבדה is introduced, it stands for all or a portion of the Levites' removal tasks (definitions 2 and 3). That עבדה means removal is immediately apparent from its absence in the enumeration of the priests' duties: they have guard duty (משמרת) but no עבדה (Num. 3:38). Surely, this cannot mean that the priests perform no cultic acts![229] The only conclusion must be that עבדה, at least in this pericope, refers exclusively to the task of moving the Tabernacle.

---

[227] See Num. 4:3, 23 et al.; Num. 8:24f.; 1 Chron. 23:24, 27; (cf. 2 Chron. 31:17; Ezra 3:8).

[228] Already anticipated by *Sifre Zuta* (Num. 8:26): "ועבדה לא יעבד: This refers to the (Levitic) porterage in the wilderness."

[229] See Num. 18:7 and n. 275.

§ 56. *Numbers, chapter 4.* The major focus, however, is upon chapter 4 where the greatest clustering of עבדה is found. Indeed, all three definitions are present, especially number 3: עבדה as a subdivision of Tabernacle removal. Where עבדה stands in apposition to porterage (משא), it assumes the more restricted meaning of dismantling and reassembling the Tabernacle (definition 3a), i.e., all removal labors except porterage. All these passages are included in the composite of all the Levitic עבדה passages (§ 64), to which the reader is referred. However, a word on the linguistic structure is in order. The apposition of עבדה–משא is expressed by three different idioms. It can take the simple form, e.g., איש איש על עבדתו ועל משאו "according to his packing and porterage" (Num. 4:49, cf. v. 19). The compound also appears: זאת עבדת . . . לעבד ולמשא "These are the tasks of . . . as to packing and porterage" (Num. 4:24, cf. vv. 27, 31), where the first עבדה is a general term for physical labor and the second, distinct from porterage, refers to specific work of dismantling and replacing the heavy curtains and planks. Lastly there is the more complex passage: כל הבא לעבד עבדת עבדה ועבדת משא באהל מועד (Num. 4:47). Once it is recognized that עבדה (absolute) and משא are in complementary apposition, there is no difficulty in rendering the passage, as follows: "all who were summoned to do the packing work and porterage work for the Tent of Meeting."

Why all this verbiage? Is this pleonastic inexactness or the contrary, technical precision? The answer surfaces as soon as it is recognized that this complementary apposition of עבדה–משא occurs only in Gershonite and Merarite passages or in summaries which include them (Num. 4:24, 27, 31, 47, 49). For the simple, uncontestable fact remains that these two clans have no porterage (משא) duties at all. The planks and curtains assigned them are carried by ox-cart.[230] Loading and unloading them is the extent of their removal toil so that the term עבדה, in their case, is reserved exclusively to their labors to make and break camp.

§ 57. *Clan distinctions.* Two more passages help clinch the case. After the Tabernacle curtains are assigned to the Gershonites as their removal task (Num. 4:21–27a), we read: "You shall make them responsible במשמרת (for guarding) all משא (their porterage)" (v. 27b).[231] The word עבדה which, as noted, prolifer-

---

[230] Even if the Levites are to furnish the drivers, how many would be needed? 2,630 Gershonites and 3,200 Merarites load and unload only six carts (Num. 7:7f.)!

[231] The LXX reads במשמרת > בשמות as in v. 32 and is accepted by most modern commentators. The emendation is not only unnecessary but wrong. The obvious purpose of listing objects by name is for taking inventory. This would be essential for the numerous attachments of the Tabernacle planks and pillars, e.g., sockets, pegs, bars, cords—all under Merarite charge (Num. 4:30f.). The Gershonites, on the other hand, had only the Tabernacle curtains as their removal duty, few in number and large in size; their loss or misplacement would be inconceivable. Moreover, the text itself militates against the emendation. Just as the Merarites' objects are borne by cart and

ates throughout the chapter, is missing here and משמרת stands in its place. No longer is it a puzzle: the furnishings, carried by carts, require no labor (עבדה), only safeguarding (משמרת).[232] Moreover, the Merarite role in Tabernacle transport is called משמרת משאם "the guarding of their porterage" (vv. 31, 32). Once again עבדה is missing. The reason is clear: no physical labor is involved.[233]

The passages dealing with the Kohathites provide final confirmation for this finding. It seems to have been overlooked that עבדה for the Kohathite is precisely the opposite of the עבדה of their brother clans. Whereas the Tabernacle's planks and curtains are transported on ox-carts, leaving the Gershonites and Merarites no porterage duties, the sacred objects—the specific charge of the Kohathites—must be carried by shoulder. And contrariwise, whereas the brother clans concentrate upon dismantling and reassembling, the Kohathites must have this work done for them by priests (Num. 4:4–15).[234] It is therefore to be expected that Kohathite עבדה, rather than being the complement of משא, should become its synonym. This is precisely what appears: their labor *is* their porterage. Let us note the following:

In regard to the princes' gifts of draught carts and oxen, Moses is told: "Accept these from them לעבד את עבדת (to *transport*)[235] the Tent of Meeting and give them to the Levites according to their respective tasks. . . . But to the

---

need only guarding during their transport, so the Gershonites' objects. Therefore, the expression משמרת משא, given twice for the Merarites (4:31, 32), is needed at least once for the Gershonites!

[232] The concluding verse (v. 28) is most likely wrongly punctuated by the Massorites. The *ethnaḥta* should be moved to ומשמרתם giving a parallel structure to the Merarites (v. 33). We should expect the task of removal as well as guard duty to be under Ithamar's jurisdiction for both clans.

[233] Num. 4:32*b* now translates, "You shall list by name the objects of their porterage watch." Haran, "The Priestly Image," 222, n. 72, deduces from his reconstruction of Tabernacle taboos that משמרת in Num. 3 (vv. 25, 31, 36) cannot refer to the Tabernacle at rest but only in transit. His reasoning is correct for it is now corroborated by the text itself: (1) Thrice we find in ch. 3 that משמרת precedes the enumerated objects and is concluded by ול(ל)כל עבדתו (for the use of ל, see n. 237). Since we have shown that the latter refers to removal so must the former (see further, § 58). (2) True, in the description of the priests' responsibility (v. 38), the camp is clearly at rest and not in motion. However, we have already pointed to the exceptional nature of this verse since the word עבדה itself is missing. Moreover, as Haran has argued (ibid.), the exclusive use of participles in v. 38, e.g., חנים (cf. יחנו vv. 23, 29), points to the ongoing priestly role in the camp and not just on the march. (3) Finally, in ch. 4 where the tasks of the labor force are minutely defined, the same objects referred to in ch. 3 as משמרת are now expanded to משמרת משא.

[234] "Aaron is 'most sacred' (2 Chron. 23:13) and the Ark is 'most sacred' and they do not harm each other. The Kohathites, however, are not 'most sacred' and are harmed by the Ark and all the interior objects which are 'most sacred'" (Num. R 19). These distinctions are further analyzed by Haran, ibid.

[235] That the oxen and carts perform עבדה is, of course, another proof that the term can only mean transport.

Kohathites he did not give any; since theirs was עבדת הקדש (the *transport* of the sacred objects), ישאו (their porterage) was by shoulder" (Num. 7:5, 9). עבדה, here, admits of no other meaning than "transport." The equation of עבדה = transport, for the Kohathite is, moreover, expressly stated by the text. The Kohathite duties are framed by these words: "This is עבדת (the *transport* obligation) of the Kohathites relating to the Tent of Meeting: ... These things are משא (the porterage) of the Kohathites relating to the Tent of Meeting" (Num. 4:4, 15*b*). Clearly עבדה here is a synonym for משא. Furthermore, in the long section itemizing the *labor* of the Kohathites (Num. 4:1–20), the sacred objects are never called their משמרת, as is the case with the furnishings assigned the Gershonites and Merarites (cf. supra), but only their משא. So indeed should it be: the brother clans have only to guard their objects during transport but the Kohathites are charged with their porterage. Thus, the premise of all the Kohathite passages is consistently the same: their משא is their עבדה.

§ 58. *The censuses.* Finally, I turn to the census of Numbers, chapter 4. That only physically qualified males are numbered is underscored by the seven-fold statement that the census was limited to ages thirty to fifty: thrice in the introductions (vv. 2, 23, 30), thrice in the sums (vv. 35, 39, 43), and once in the grand total (v. 47). The last is the complex-structured עבדה clause, already discussed (§ 56), on which one more observation is in order. For having grasped P's terminology of Levitic עבדה—labor, in general, and removal, in particular—it is possible to penetrate to the intent of the verse and see that it could not have been expressed in any other way. It sums up the physical work assigned all the Levite clans as: עבדת עבדה "packing work" (Gershonites and Merarites) and עבדת משא "porterage work" (Kohathites).

An unexpected boon resulting from the analysis of Levitic עבדה is new insight into the literary structure of the two censuses of Numbers, chapters 3 and 4.[236] Having seen that chapter 4 stresses עבדה, the physical labor assigned to the Levites, the different formulation used in the first Levitic census, Numbers 3:14–39, can be accounted for. The framework for each clan reads: משמרת ... וכל/לכל עבדתו (3:25f., 31, 36, cf. 38).[237] Thus, priorities are switched: משמרת is no

---

[236] Once and for all, the view that Num. 4 is a doublet of 3:14–39 (e.g., G. von Rad [supra n. 3] 89–93) must be abandoned. Indeed, once עבדה, משמרת and קרב are properly translated, many hoary "cruxes" disappear: e.g., 4:5–16 is no "*Einschub*"; 4:17–20 is not a "*Nachtrag*" alluding to a Kohathite "*Untergang*"; 18:3*b* does not contradict 1:50 etc. (despite Gunneweg 151, 180f., and K. Möhlenbrink "Die levitischen Überlieferungen des Alten Testaments" *ZAW* [1934] 52, N.F. 11:184–231, esp. 224f., upon whose analysis of Num. 4 Gunneweg relies).

[237] The equation וכל = לכל has yet to be demonstrated. My view is that the *lamed* is clearly not a preposition but a conjunctive with emphatic force, best rendered by "including." Provisionally, see P. Joüon's *Grammaire de l'Hébreu Biblique* (1965), § 125, 1.1, 2, and infra n. 279. The possibility that the *lamed* is a pure emphatic particle should not be discounted, see P. Haupt, quoted by G-K-C, 143e, and infra n. 262.

longer the afterthought it was in chapter 4 (Num. 4:27, 28, 31,[238] 32), but the main subject and the main word, outnumbering the occurrences of עבדה seven to three. The reason for the stress on משמרת is that guard duty has no age qualification. All Levites counted must serve, not only the elderly (so explicitly, Num. 8:25f.) but in theory, even the very young, age one month and up.[239] Indeed, it seems that from P's viewpoint, all but infants perform some guard duty or are in training for it. In any event, since many more Levites are involved in guard duty (according to the census nearly two-thirds) than in actual labor, משמרת receives the main stress in the full Levitic census of Numbers, chapter 3. Moreover, of the two major Levitic roles, guarding and removal, there can be no doubt which is the more important: the labor force is activated only when the camp is on the move, but guard duty is a perpetual responsibility. Indeed, when the Levites are apportioned their share of the Midianite spoils, twice the text emphasizes that they are שמרי משמרת המשכן (Num. 31:30, 47). Thus, the Levites are rewarded specifically for their service as Tabernacle guards.

§ 59. *Recapitulation.* Levitic עבדה has been found to mean the physical labor of Tabernacle removal. With guard duty (משמרת) it constitutes the main work assigned to the Levites by the Priestly source.[240] The term עבדה in Numbers, chapter 4, can also refer to the specific labors designated to the Levite clans, either as a complement to or a synonym of porterage (משא). In the case of Gershonite and Merarite clans who have no porterage, their עבדה refers to their laborious task of dismantling and reassembling the Tabernacle complex. The Kohathites, on the other hand, are exempt from the latter, but are exclusively engaged in the transport of the sacred objects by shoulder. The common denominator of all these usages is that עבדה will refer to that aspect of the Levites' work which requires heavy labor.

§ 60. *Numbers 4:19b and the LXX.* The inevitable "fly in the ointment" appears here. Concerning the Kohathites we read: "assign them על עבדתו ואל משאו." If, as claimed, the Kohathite labor consisted solely of porterage then the משא should suffice, and עבדה would be superfluous. The LXX, however, unambiguously translates one term for the two; it seems that על עבדתו was not in the translator's Hebrew text. Moreover, it is simple to account for the gloss; the copyist's eye or memory fastened upon the chapter's concluding verse where the same formulation occurs (4:49).

---

[238] Even here משמרת is preceded by עבדה in the previous verse. See The Composite, § 64 ad loc.

[239] According to Ehrlich, *Randglossen* (on Exod. 30:12), the vocabulary of the two censuses points to another distinction: ראש is used in the counting of the able-bodied males (Exod. 30:12; Num. 1:2, 4:1, 21, 26:1) but not in the census for the entire people (Num. 3:15, 40). This leads him to render ראש as "der Korn."

[240] See supra n. 226 for a qualified third.

Q.E.D.? Not at all. As S. Daniel observes,[241] the Septuagint renders משא here by 'αναφορά a rare word, one never again used for משא. We, therefore, have no right to conclude that the translators had before them a Hebrew text which omitted על עבדתו. The likelihood is that their *Vorlage* was the same as the Masoretic text, and what the LXX has bequeathed us is not translation but interpretation. The Alexandrians may have been as sensitive as we to the difficulties involved in assigning the Kohathites additional עבדה. Their solution was to regard the compound על עבדתו ואל משאו as a hendiadys, the equivalent perhaps of עבדת משא (v. 47) which we interpreted earlier as the Kohathite share of the Tabernacle labors. Indeed since Kohathite עבדה is identical with משא, the use of hendiadys is semantically as well as grammatically possible,[242] and the Septuagint reading points the way.[243]

§ 61. *Post-conquest* עבדה. The instances of Levitic עבדה still awaiting discussion are Numbers 8:11, 15, 19, 22, 16:9, 18:4, 6, 21, 23, 31. In all these passages the specific Levitic tasks are no longer identified and itemized as in chapters 3 and 4, and therefore עבדה will invariably mean either "physical labor" (definition 1) or "removal" (definition 2), in general. Whatever comment need be made on individual verses in this group is reserved for The Composite, § 64. Numbers, chapter 18, however, is singularly rich in new ideas and enigmas and merits extended treatment. The first two verses (18:4, 6) present no particular difficulty;[244] Numbers 18:21, 23, 31 do. Their problem is not primarily philological but historical. This is a new time setting. Here and here alone, P projects Levitic עבדה into the future. Henceforth, in the post-conquest period, Levites will receive tithes in return for their עבדה. As to the makeup of their future עבדה, this text and, indeed, all of P is silent, and one must make his own deductions. However, the new understanding of the term עבדה can aid. The possible solutions are narrowed down to two. The first and most obvious is that with Israel's

---

241 *Recherches sur le vocabulaire du culte dans le Septante* (1966) 76–87.

242 עבדה can be a synonym for משא (see Num. 3:31, 7:9).

243 We would be remiss to neglect the importance of the Septuagint which, to our knowledge, is the only version that does not uniformly render עבדה by "service" but resorts frequently to "work." The stems, respectively, are λειτουργ- and ἐργ- and are thoroughly investigated by Daniel. Interestingly enough, she concludes that the former stem is the general term whereas the latter refers to specific labors. However, other distinctions implied by the stems (e.g., loftiness versus menial, etc.) are not borne out by our study (e.g., n. 272 on Num. 16:9). Nonetheless, the acknowledgment by the LXX that Levitic עבדה has a primary meaning of physical labor is significant.

Perhaps we should also not sell short the Targums, which invariably render פולחן ("cult") since the latter's etymology is the root "to work" just as Hebrew עבדה. פולחן as "labor" is certainly attested, e.g., T. Ezek. 39:18. Thus, the possibility exists that the Aramaic translators were aware of עבדה as labor, but since פולחן can mean "work" or "cult" we can never be sure.

244 If עבדה and משמרת are both blithely translated as "*Dienst*" (see inter alia, von Rad, 113–116), Num. 18:1–7 turns into a jumble. See our discussion, § 64, nn. 273–277.

wanderings terminated, the need for a movable sanctuary has also ended. Only guard duty is left as the major Levitic office.[245] Indeed, it is for their service in protecting the sanctuary against the incursions of the unauthorized that they are awarded dues of annual tithes.[246] If this solution is correct then עבדה will have assumed a fourth meaning: it would now be restricted to guard duty, a synonym for משמרת, a usage it did not have before.

However, a second solution is possible: Levitic עבדה continues unchanged in the Promised Land. As is well known, P does not project beyond the conquest and immediate settlement. It says nothing about the replacement of the Tabernacle by some permanent structure or about the selection of its permanent site. Rather than assume with the critics that P takes both structure and site for

---

[245] משמרת is also a function of שרת, e.g., 1:50*b* ‖ 1:53*b*; 3:6*b*, 7*a*; 18:2*a* ‖ 18:3*a*; 8:26. That the שרת has guarding functions, see Exod. 33:11 (E): "ומשרתו, Joshua the son of Nun, נער, would not stir out of the tent." For the possibility that נער is a soldier in Ugaritic and Egyptian, see Gordon, *Ugaritic Textbook*, Glossary, no. 1666.

Whatever the original meaning of שרת (most likely "to serve") its biblical contexts betray multiple meanings to cover multiple historically developed institutions. Thus priests "officiate" (in which case the direct object is rarely used) whereas Levites "guard" the Tabernacle and "assist" the laity and the priesthood (the direct object always being used). In any case, the usual translation "minister" (e.g., Eerdmans, 122f.) is inadequate.

[246] We cannot accept Y. Kaufmann's thesis, *Toledot ha-Emuna ha-Yisraelit*, I, 154–157 [abridg.-trans. M. Greenberg, 190f.], that the Levitic tithe of Numbers, in contrast to the tithe demanded by Deuteronomy, is voluntary: (1) The key verbs are נתתי (18:21, 24, 26) and תקחו (vv. 26, 28). The Levites are not dependent upon the philanthropic whim of the landowner, but they may seize that which has been assigned to them, i.e., one-tenth of each yearly crop. That תקחו means "take possession" is well attested (e.g., in P alone: for property, Lev. 25:36; Num. 3:47, 31:30; marriage, Lev. 20:14, 17, 21, 21:13, 14). (2) The tithe is "given" in reward for work (עבדה, 18:21, 31). Just as the latter is perennial and unceasing, so must be the former. Moreover, the tithe is called שכר (v. 31), which in עבדה contexts can only mean "wages" (e.g., Gen. 30:28f.; Deut. 15:18; Ezek. 29:18, etc.). (3) A logical consideration: Since no other emoluments but the tithes are assigned the Levites, on what does P expect them to live once the manna ceases? (4) Even the priestly tithe of Lev. 27:30, I suspect, is yearly and compulsory and the text should translate, "Every tenth of the land (yield)." Moreover, the cattle which "pass under the shepherd's staff" (v. 32) are not for purposes of tithe but for daily inventory when they exit from and return to their pens. Its rendering, therefore, should be "Every tenth of the herd and the flock—of whatever passes under the shepherd's staff—shall be holy to the Lord."

Thus, I submit, "for the tithes set aside by the Israelites as a contribution to the Lord" (Num. 18:24) clearly implies that originally the tithes accrued "to the Lord," i.e., to the priests, in keeping with Lev. 27:30ff., and as the priestly dues (תרומה) continue to do (see 18:8, 12, 19, 26, 28, 28, 29). Num. 18:21ff., then, is a later development than Lev. 27:30ff. Dues originally assigned to the priesthood are now transferred to the Levites in compensation for their labors at the Sanctuary. This transfer, however, only applies to the land tithe; the animal tithe is forgotten and it never crops up in legislation again.

granted, let us follow the simpler reading of the text that P does not regard the conquest as the terminus ad quem for the Tabernacle [247] and, by the same token, it assumes that the Tabernacle will continue to function qua Tabernacle, as a portable, mobile shrine. Is there any evidence for this view in Scripture? The answer is strongly in the affirmative.

§ 62. *Samuel.* The text of 2 Samuel 7:6f. (= 1 Chron. 17:5f.), generally conceded as historically reliable, [248] relates of contemporary opposition to the building of Jerusalem's Temple on the grounds that Israel's God had heretofore neither dwelt in a Temple nor requested one. Rather, "I continued to move about in a Tabernacle-Tent. All the time I moved about among the Israelites ..." [249] Not only does this text state unequivocally that before David the Deity resided in a Tabernacle-type structure but that it functioned as such: it "moved about." [250] According to this ancient tradition, then, the Tabernacle was a viable, operative institution in the settled land. [251]

---

[247] Here I follow Haran, "Shilo and Jerusalem," *JBL* (1962) 81:14–24, but differ with his reading of 2 Sam. 7, as the discussion will show.

[248] E.g., Noth holds that 2 Sam. 7 is a unified composition and is pre-Solominic: "David and Israel in 2 Sam. 7," *The Laws in the Pentateuch and Other Studies* (1966) 250–259.

[249] The following exegetical notes are the most relevant: ואהיה מתהלך "expresses forcibly the idea of continuance," S. R. Driver, *Notes on the Hebrew Text of the Books of Samuel* (ed.², 1913), ad loc. I take באהל ובמשכן as a hendiadys. According to P, the tent and tabernacle are, respectively, the outer and inner cover of the sanctuary (Exod. 40:19); the ב is instrumental. בכל בני ישראל: Chronicles reads "among Israel," but the Samuel text is preferable.

[250] The *hithpaʿel* of הלך means "to move about." With God as the subject, its clearest examplar is in the Eden story: "The sound of the Lord God moving about (מתהלך) among the trees of the garden" (Gen. 3:8 [J]). This notion of God's mobility is fundamental to the Deuteronomist, e.g., "Since the Lord your God moves about (מתהלך) in your camp to protect you" (Deut. 23:15). The presence of God is not confined to the sanctuary. (It is only God's *name* which is "tabernacled" in the central sanctuary.) Nor is it attached to the Ark, for as the end of the above-cited verse expressly states: "let your camp be holy; let Him not find anything unseemly among you and turn away from you." Thus, in D, the presence of God moves about the people, unbound by the sanctuary or its sancta.

For P, however, God's presence is coextensive with His Tabernacle; once He leaves it, it is destroyed. Actually P and D are not far apart; both aver that holiness within the Israelite society is the sine qua non for God's protecting presence. In my study of impurities, I hope to demonstrate that according to P's theology sin/impurity within the community registers upon the sanctuary, and when a critical point is reached God must leave. P's concept is the more anthropomorphic and pagan and is closer to the form of God's indwelling presupposed by 2 Sam. 7:6f.; "I continued to move about in a Tabernacle-Tent."

Another instance of התהלך provides the closest analogue to Samuel: ונתתי משכני בתוככם ··· והתהלכתי בתוככם (Lev. 26:11f.). If, as in the rest of P, משכן is God's earthly abode, then it is the means by which God's presence is felt throughout the land.

True, the testimony of 2 Samuel 7 has been discredited by the flat contradiction of 1 Samuel 1–3 which speaks of a Temple at Shilo within which the Ark was enshrined. The contradiction, I submit, is more apparent than real. P's own history ends with the Tabernacle settled in Shilo at the end of Joshua's days (Josh. 18:1). Moreover, there are traditions from other hands which place the Ark in Gilgal (Josh. 3f.), Shechem (Josh. 8:30ff.), Bethel (Jud. 20:27f.), Shilo (1 Sam. 1–3), and in Israel's war camp against the Philistines (1 Sam. 4–7) and the Ammonites (2 Sam. 11:11).[252] That the Ark was sheltered in a tent and that, concomitantly, the tent contained other cultic paraphernalia are assumptions in keeping with extra-biblical evidence, particularly the *qubba* of pre-Islamic nomads, and I would agree wholeheartedly with de Vaux's conclusion "we ought not to separate the Ark and the Tent, . . . the Priestly description of the desert sanctuary . . . did preserve an authentic tradition."[253]

If, then, the Ark was always enshrined in a Tabernacle-tent, it is easy to account for the existence of a tradition that full Levitic עבדה, as known in the Wilderness, persisted in Canaan until the destruction of Shilo. This tradition would resolve the crux of Shilo for it would allow for the side-by-side coexistence of both Temple and Tabernacle, the latter reserved for war emergencies as well

---

Indeed, since this verse is part of P(H)'s projection into post-conquest conditions, it may envisage a circuit-riding Tabernacle in the settled land. In any event, it should be clear that the image of the Tabernacle in Samuel corresponds in language and concept with Lev. 26 and not with any other source, and is another indication that the opponents of the Jerusalem Temple, as reflected in 2 Sam. 7, based themselves on a Tabernacle-centered theology, precisely as we find in P. (I am grateful to M. Greenberg for indicating to me that my interpretation of מתהלך is supported by A. E. Speiser, "The Durative Hithpaʿel: A *tān*-Form," *JAOS* [1955] 75:52–55.)

[251] This thesis finds support in Ps. 78:28, "He let them (the birds) fall in the midst of His camp, all around His Tabernacle." (For the singular meaning of משכנת see Ps. 43:3, 84:2, 132:5, 7 [‖מקום]; Job 18:21 [‖מקום]; 39:6 [‖בית]; Ug. texts [Gordon] 128:III:19; 2 Aqht:V:32f.; and see Ug. Grammar § 13.17.) The psalmist, it will be noted, uses P's concept of the Tabernacle in the center of the camp, and yet by all accounts this psalm is old! (E.g., 10th cent., Eissfeldt, *Das Lied Moses, BAL* [1958] 36f.; 9th cent., G. E. Wright, "The Controversy of God: A Form Critical Study of Deuteronomy 32," *Essays Muilenberg* [1962] 26–67.) See also the discussion of the Tabernacle Psalms in V. W. Rabe, "The Temple as Tabernacle" (1963) 20–62, esp. on Ps. 78, 59f. Also, note the startling resemblances of the dimensions of the Arad sanctuary and altar to their Tabernacle counterparts; see Aharoni, op. cit., 25 and supra, n. 166.

[252] The Ark was also with David at the beginning of Absolom's rebellion, but only momentarily (2 Sam. 15:24–29).

[253] *Ancient Israel*, 302; idem, "Arche d'Alliance et Tente de Réunion," *Mémorial A Gelin* (1961) 55–70. For the latest summary on the origin of the Ark, see H. Davies, "The Ark of the Covenant," *ASTI* (1966–1967) 5:30–47. He concurs that the Ark goes back to the wilderness sojourn; however, deducing it from a reconstruction of JE (Exod. 33:5*b*–7) is highly questionable.

as for peacetime circuits among the people.[254] It would account for David's housing the Ark in a tent when he brought it to Jerusalem, not that he could not find it an adequate house but that he was returning to the living Wilderness tradition, suspended only two generations earlier with the destruction of Shilo.[255] It would explain P's silence about the site of the Tabernacle and its replacement by a Temple, because P knew that the Tabernacle was the authentic tradition until vitiated by Nathan's prophecy to David.[256]

---

[254] It might throw light on the apparent "movable" center of Israel's early Federation: Gilgal, Shechem, Shilo, Bethel. Thus, Israel might gather at any hallowed spot and the Ark and its Tabernacle be brought there. Would this be the meaning of "in every place where I cause my name to be mentioned I will come to you and bless you" (Exod. 20:21b)?

[255] So F. M. Cross, "The Priestly Tabernacle," *BA* (1947) 10:45–68 (reprinted in *The Biblical Archaeologist Reader*, I, 201–228, followed by V. W. Rabe. The major support for the alleged lateness of P's Tabernacle has been the assumption that the Tabernacle's ornamentation and design were inspired by Solomon's Temple (so most recently, Haran, "Shilo and Jerusalem," *JBL* [1962] 81:14–17, 23f.). As J. A. Scott has shown, *The Pattern of the Tabernacle* (1965), the many basic dissimilarities between the Temple and the Tabernacle in both dimension and material militate against the theory of imitation. Furthermore, Cross may be correct that P preserved the last Tabernacle to survive, i.e., David's Tent, which obviously was more lavish than its Wilderness predecessor.

[256] T. E. Fretheim's challenging article, "The Priestly Document: Anti-Temple?" *VT* (1968) 18:313–329, was published too late to be assimilated into the body of this study. He accepts the thesis of M. Noth, *The History of Israel* (1958) 91, that the Ark had no permanent resting place but was "set up in one place for a more or less prolonged period of time and this place formed the central place of worship." Only whereas Noth ascribes the Ark's mobility to the fear lest it "should become the object of a local cult after the manner of the Canaanites" (ibid., 94), Fretheim sees the motivation, as I do, in P's ideological rejection of a fixed Temple. I differ with Fretheim, however, in his chronological assumptions and, hence, in the conclusions he derives from them. For example, since he presumes a post-586 date for the composition as well as editing of P, he is forced to scrounge for evidence of opposition to the building of the second Temple. His results are meager and uncompelling.

Jeremiah can only be made over into an antagonist to the institution of the Temple, per se, by declaring spurious all contradictory verses in his book (e.g., 3:17, 14:21, 17:12, 31:5, 33:18–22). Moreover, that Jeremiah did not foresee the rebuilding of the Temple is no great conundrum. All his restoration prophecies are directed to the exiles of 721 and 597; none date after 586 (not even in chs. 30–31). Therefore, whenever Jeremiah speaks of ingathering, the Temple is still standing! As for Isa. 66:1f., the opposition is not directed to the Temple but to its devotees. (By Fretheim's logic, since sacrifice is condemned in v. 3, are we to suppose that the prophet projected a non-sacrificial cult? And what of v. 6, not to speak of vv. 18b, 20, 21, 23, which predicate the Temple and its ritual?). The objections to the Temple in both Jeremiah and Isaiah are nothing more than variations on a ubiquitous prophetic theme: rite without ethics is worthless. (E.g., see J. Muilenberg's discussion, *Isaiah, chs. 40–66* [Interpreter's Bible 1956] V, 758–760.) It is also significant that Noth, who also posits opposition to the building of the second Temple, cites the Samaritan schism as his only proof!

§ 63. *Chronicles*. Finally, is it not by this tradition that it is possible to explain how the Chronicler interpreted the P source before him? Twice he informs us that the porterage work of the Levites ceased only with the construction of Jerusalem's Temple (1 Chron. 23:25f.; 2 Chron. 35:3).[257] In other words, the Chronicler assumes that until the time of David, Levitic עבדה continued to include duties of transport.[258]

("Jerusalem and the Israelite Tradition," *The Laws*..., 143.) Indeed, Haran has argued more cogently from Isa. 66 that the Temple was not yet rebuilt, and the prophet's opening words are not a rebuke but a consolation to those whose efforts to rebuild the Temple have not prevailed, *Between Ri'shonōt and Ḥadashōt* (1963) 94–96 (Heb.).

Furthermore, the post-exilic era is uniquely distinguished by its attempt to harmonize conflicting legal and cultic traditions, especially those in P and D. (For the best analysis to date, see Y. Kaufmann, *Toledot* IV, 324–353.) This means that the laws of P were regarded as God's word as much as the already promulgated laws of D. If P were intended as a blueprint for the second Temple, is it then conceivable that such essential sancta as the anointment oil, the altar of wood and metal, the Urim and Tummim, and above all the Ark with its attendant *kappōret* and cherubim, would have been omitted from the rebuilt Temple with nary a midrashic explanation in our post-exilic texts?

The dating of the cultic materials of P (again, their composition, not their compilation and redaction) must be sought in pre-exilic times; but to demonstrate this a separate study will be required.

[257] Haran, "The Disappearance of the Ark," *IEJ* (1963) 13:52f., is surely correct in believing that 2 Chron. 35:3 is unhistorical. Indeed, it is to be seen as a midrash on Num. 7:9 where משא ישאו‖בכתף בכתף but where three changes have been introduced: (a) Ark porterage, a Kohathite function, is ascribed to all Levites; (b) עבדה is reinterpreted as "cult service" as elsewhere in Chronicles (e.g., 1 Chron. 23:28. For the translation of Num. 6:7 see ad loc. § 64, and § 73, for a similar midrash in Nehemiah); (c) the Levites are a consecrated class (קדושים) contra to P (see 2 Chron. 23:6 and § 7). However, I agree with Rudolph ad loc., versus Haran, that this verse does not imply that the Ark was transported (in cultic processions) during the period of the first Temple, since it would contradict the Chronicler's own assertion that Ark porterage ceased in David's time (1 Chron. 23:26). On the negative evidence of Ps. 132, see now D. R. Hillers, "Ritual Procession of the Ark and Ps. 132," *CBQ* (1968) 30:48–55. Moreover, תנו, as recognized by Ehrlich, *Randglossen*, ad loc., can mean "leave" (e.g., Hos. 5:4) and the sense of 2 Chron. 35:3, with Rudolph (also cited by Haran, ibid., nn. 12, 15), is that ever since the erection of the Temple the Levites have been relieved of their Ark-carrying role and are therefore free to assume new cultic responsibilities. Indeed, in Josiah's time, according to the Chronicler, they permanently replace the laity as ritual slaughterers of the Pesach (2 Chron. 35:6, 11).

[258] When the reorganization of the cult took place and the Levites were assigned new duties (1 Chron. 23:27–32). Of course, the Chronicler's Tabernacle theory leads to fanciful reconstruction: the Ark was brought to Jerusalem but the Tabernacle and bronze altar remained at Gibeon (1 Chron. 1:3–6; also 1 Chron. 16:39f., 21:29); an angel prevented David from worshipping at Gibeon (1 Chron. 21:30), but the theophany at Araunah's altar (1 Chron. 21:26) led David to declare the latter as the future site of the Temple (2 Chron. 22:1). In my opinion, it was the memory of a functioning Tabernacle in the pre-Shilo period that led to the natural, if forced, variant tradition that the Tabernacle continued to operate until Solomon's Temple.

Thus, for P, the post-conquest cult would continue the same, with only one slight difference. In the Wilderness, the Ark moved with the people; in the settlement, it moved among them. In either case, it remained in their midst. The עבדה of the Levites made this possible.

§ 64. *Composite of Levitic* עבדה. The results of this study are best summarized through a composite of all the passages of Levitic עבדה in translation. Parentheses are used for the identification of pronouns and comment is reserved for the notes. The category of עבדה in each passage (see definitions, § 53) is indicated by the following bracketed sigla: G = physical labor, in general (definition 1); R = total removal labor (definition 2); R_{da} = the dismantling-assembling division of removal, rendered for convenience as "packing" (definition 3a); R_t = transport division of removal (definition 3b).

Num. 3:7	They (the Levites) shall perform guard duty for him (Aaron) and for the whole community before the Tent of Meeting in doing[259] the work [G] of the Tabernacle.
Num. 3:8	They (the Levites) shall guard all the furnishings of the Tent of Meeting—a guard duty on behalf of the Israelites—in doing the work [G] of the Tabernacle.[260]
Num. 3:25f.	The guard duty of the Gershonites for[261] the Tent of Meeting comprised: . . .—including[262] their removal [R].[263]
Num. 3:31	Their guard duty (the Kohathites): . . .—including their removal [R].*
Num. 3:36	The allotted guard duty of the Merarites: . . .—including their removal [R].*

---

[259] See G-K-C, § 114, 0; Joüon, § 124, 0.

[260] This verse does not "define the preceding one" (SB) nor should 8*b* be deleted (BH). Both vv. 7 and 8 are necessary for spelling out the total guard duty incumbent upon the Levites, i.e., when the camp is at rest (v. 7) and in transit (v. 8). The latter is made certain by 8*aα* referring to the sancta, which the Levites guarded during the march (Num. 3:25, 31, 36 and see § 58) but which only priests were allowed to guard in camp (Num. 18:5). The Levitic guard duty when the camp was at rest took place around the Tabernacle complex (Num. 1:53). For this very reason, עבדה in this verse (but not in v. 7) might well refer to removal labor (R). It would definitely be the case if the first לעבד את עבדת המשכן (v. 7*b*) could be proven a dittography of the second (v. 8*b*), but the evidence of the textual manuscripts and versions is negative.

[261] ב = relating to, in connection with, for. See G-K-C, § 119h; Joüon, § 133c.

[262] See supra n. 234 on וכל/ל. The possibility also must be considered that both the *waw* and *lamed* are for emphasis and עבדה = G, leading to the translation "whatever this work [G]," in accordance with 3:7 and 8.

[263] In truth, עבדה for Kohathites = R_t and for Gershonites and Merarites (vv. 25, 36) = R_{da}. But since these distinctions are not given till the following chapter, only the overall job of moving the Tabernacle (or work in general, see n. 262) is meant.

* See n. 263.

Num. 4:4	These are the tasks [R$_t$] of the Kohathites for the Tent of Meeting: the most sacred objects.
Num. 4:19	. . . each of them (the Kohathites) according to his porterage work [G].[264]
Num. 4:23f.	. . . all who qualify[265] to serve in the work [R] force[266] for the Tent of Meeting. These are the tasks [R] of the Merarite clans as to packing [R$_{da}$] and porterage.
Num. 4:27f.	All the work [R] of the Gershonites—all their packing [R$_{da}$] and porterage—shall be performed on orders from Aaron and his sons. . . . Those are the tasks [R] of the Gershonites for the Tent of Meeting and their guard duty,[267] under Ithamar son of Aaron the priest.
Num. 4:30f., 33	. . . all who are admitted to the work [R] force for the Tent of Meeting. Their porterage which they shall guard,[268] inclusive of their packing [R$_{da}$] labor for the Tent of Meeting, shall comprise: . . . Those are the tasks [R] of the Merarite clans—all their work [G] for the Tent of Meeting.
Num. 4:35(39, 43)	. . . all who were admitted* to the work [R] force for the Tent of Meeting.
Num. 4:47	. . . all who were admitted* to do the packing [R$_{da}$] work [G] and porterage work [G] for the Tent of Meeting.[269]
Num. 4:49	. . . according to his packing [R$_{da}$] and porterage.
Num. 7:5, 9	Accept these (oxen) from them (the princes) to transport [R$_t$][270] the Tent of Meeting and give them to the Levites according to their respective jobs [R]. . . . But to the Kohathites he did not give any; since theirs was the transport [R$_t$] of the sacred objects their porterage was by shoulder.

---

[264] For the probable hendiadys see § 60.

[265] בוא is the opposite of שוב (8:25). They are technical terms regarding qualifications for the Levite movers of the Tabernacle. Hence, "qualify," or "be admitted" and "be retired," respectively.

[266] The "work force" refers exclusively to the physical labors in moving the Tabernacle. It is usually expressed by a simple hendiadys לצבא לעבדה (4:39, 43) or its variations (4:30; 8:24 and here). Cf. עבדה—משא, § 56.

[267] See n. 232.

[268] See § 57.

[269] See §§ 56, 58.

[270] See n. 235.

* See n. 265.

Num. 8:11   . . . to perform the Lord's tasks [R].[271]

Num. 8:19(15)   . . . to perform the tasks [R] for the Tent of Meeting* on
                      behalf of the Israelites.

Num. 8:22   Thereafter the Levites qualified‡ to perform their tasks [R]
                      for the Tent of Meeting.*

Num. 8:24–26   . . . they shall qualify‡ to serve in the work [R] force for
                      the Tent of Meeting. At the age of fifty they shall be dis-
                      charged from the work [R] force and shall labor no more.
                      They shall assist their brothers in keeping guard over the
                      Tent of Meeting but they shall perform no labor [R].

Num. 16:9   Is it not enough for you that the God of Israel has set you
                      apart from the community of Israel by giving you access
                      to Him, to perform the labors [R] of the Lord's Tabernacle,
                      and to minister to the community to serve them?[272]

---

[271] I submit that עבדה in Num. ch. 8 means removal labor in all cases (vv. 11, 15,
19, 22, 24–26). This view alone can explain the need for purificatory rites accompanying the induction service of the Levites. For guard duty (משמרת) performed around
and at a distance from the Tabernacle complex would require no purification since no
contact with sancta is entailed; removal operations (עבדה), on the other hand, being
the sole Levitic function calling for the direct handling of sancta, would require
purificatory aspergings and sacrifices. Moreover, the induction ceremony is limited
only to mature Levites, for one of the purifications reads: "pass a razor over their
whole bodies" (v. 7). But physical maturity is a requirement for removal work and
not for guard duty (see §§ 54, 58). Furthermore, another purpose for משמרת is "to
remove wrath (e.g., 1:53); yet it is missing in v. 19. Hence, we have another indication
that עבדה of Num. 8 refers strictly to removal.
    Another advantage to עבדה as removal (R) would be to unite all of ch. 8 into a
single unit (despite the separate introduction, v. 23), since עבדה of the final verses
(24–26) also means removal (see § 54). Thus, ch. 8 would become a fitting conclusion
to the Levitic prescriptions within Num. 3–8; as follows: ch. 3, guard duty and complete census; ch. 4, removal labor and census for physically able Levites; ch. 7, work
tools are provided; ch. 8, work force is inducted; 8:23–26, work force is retired.
    For the impact of this view on the enigmatic ולכפר על בני ישראל (v. 19), see
§§ 27–30.
[272] See n. 226 for the meaning of the last phrase. This verse by itself gives the lie
to the accepted notion that P's Levites are menial servants and that עבדה is a euphemism for janitorial functions. To the contrary, since Levites have no access to the
Tabernacle, its upkeep is not their responsibility, but is a chore for the Priests! And
we have seen that עבדה where "access" to sancta was expressly forbidden (18:3) is
considered by P the highest privilege, as the bestowal of God's consummate grace.
Ezekiel's denigration of the Levites is sui generis; it finds no echo in post-exilic sources
and is a problem to itself, see § 73.
    עבדה still means "removal duties" (R) and excludes guarding since the latter is

* See n. 271.   ‡ See n. 265.

Num. 18:4   They (the Levites) shall be attached to you and do the
                   guard duty of the Tent of Meeting—indeed,[273] all the work
                   [G] of the Tent.[274]

Num. 18:6   . . . they (the Levites) are assigned to you in dedication to
                   the Lord to perform the work [G] of the Tent of Meet-
                   ing.[275]

---

not encompassed by the term להקריב אליו. Only removal gave the Levites access to
sancta; guarding, on the other hand, took place outside the sacred area and at the
entrance where laymen could gather (see § 12) but were warned away from sancta
(18:3). עבדה, comprising removal and guarding, may be found in ch. 18 (vv. 4, 6 and
less likely vv. 21, 23, 31, if §§ 61–63 find acceptance).

[273] See nn. 237, 262.

[274] This verse is, in thought, identical with Num. 3:7 (see n. 260). However, the
context is different. It deals solely with the assembled and functioning Tabernacle and
the need to prevent encroachment upon the sacred objects (v. 3) and upon the officiating priests (v. 4*b*). For further discussion, see §§ 13–15 and table C, § 23.

[275] That עבדה here is Levitic work, in toto, and comprises guarding as well as
removal, is indicated by the following verse (v. 7). It is clear that priestly duties (v. 7,
see infra) are contrasted with Levitic עבדה (v. 6). Just as the former includes guarding
(7*a*), so the latter.

V. 7 presents us with the only mention in all of P of priestly עבדה. Its problem is
twofold: it looks textually corrupt and ideologically indefensible. ועבדתם עבדת מתנה
אתן את כהנתכם. The commentaries admit the difficulties. Some follow the LXX, Sam.
and Syr. which read ועבדתם עבדה, but the emendation says nothing and מתנה is
attached to nothing. (Ehrlich, *Randglossen*, ad loc., retains the consonantal text
reading ועבדתם, but the words after מתנה are left dangling.)

E. A. Speiser, "Unrecognized Dedication," *IEJ* (1963) 13:69–73, breaks out of
this impasse by interpreting מתנה as "dedication" rather than previously held "gift,"
and he renders: the Levites "given (נתנים) in dedication (מתנה) to the Lord. You (the
priests), on the other hand, along with your sons, shall take care (תשמרו) to perform
(ועבדתם) your duties in all matters pertaining to the altar and what is inside the curtain.
I have made (אתן) your priesthood a service of dedication (עבדת מתנה)." Speiser's is a
giant step forward but he has not cleared the woods:

1. The proposed hendiadys תשמרו ועבדתם, eight words apart, is grammatically
awkward. Moreover, it is nonsense. The priesthood has no עבדה "inside the curtain"
(see table B). ועבדתם must therefore be detached from ושמרתם.

2. עבדת מתנה "service of dedication" is also troublesome. Nowhere is the priesthood called a מתנה or its ranks נתנים. Moreover, the root נתן, as Speiser himself
observes, connotes subordination. Priests, however, are never assigned ("subordi-
nated"); rather, assigned to them are Levites (Num. 3:9, 8:16, 19, 18:6; 1 Chron.
6:33) and emoluments (e.g., Num. 18:8, 11, 12, 19).

A tempting solution—but requiring radical amputation—is to delete ועבדתם עבדת
מתנה אתן את כהנתכם; these words are indeed missing in the parallel verse, Num. 3:10.
(The LXX, to the contrary, puts them in, but the changed vocabulary reveals the hand
of a glossator, see Daniel, 25f.). Thus, in both verses, the injunction "to guard" is now
followed logically by the penalty meted out to encroachers. The purpose of the gloss
would be simple: not to contrast with the Levites' מתנה (dedication) of the previous

Num. 18:21	. . . in return[276] for the work they do: the work [G/R] of the Tent of Meeting.[277]
Num. 18:23	The Levites alone shall perform the work [G/R] of the Tent of Meeting.*
Num. 18:31	. . . in return† for your work [G/R] for the Tent of Meeting.*

עבדה IN P

§ 65. *The Pentateuch.* Outside of the Levitic texts, P uses עבדה only eleven times more in connection with the Tabernacle. These occur in the account of the construction of the Tabernacle and merit individual examination. One verse actually speaks of Levitic עבדה, "the work of the Levites under Ithamar" (Exod. 38:21).[278] Two other verses mention כלי עבדה, "work tools" (Exod. 27:19a,

---

verse (so Speiser), but to anticipate the priests' מתנה (gifts) in the following section (vv. 8–20); the priests are rewarded for incurring mortal danger in their עבדה (note v. 1b—same term כהנתכם) just as the Levites are rewarded for their hazardous עבדה (18:2f., 21–23; and see § 23). Thus we revert to מתנה as "gift." AT's rendering "lucrative service" (following Ehrlich, *Randglossen* II, 178) is not, as Speiser contends, "hardly an edifying picture of high religious function" ("Unrecognized Dedication," p. 70), but justifiable compensation for the risk of life.

In my view, the Massoretic division and vocalization are correct: ועבדתם contrasts with תשמרו just as Levitic משמרת—עבדה (e.g., 3:31, 36); one verse (albeit abstruse) actually terminates with the verbal form ועבדו (see 4:26). That the priests had guard duty over the sancta has been established. But did they also have עבדה, physical labor? Indeed they did: to dismantle and cover the sancta when camp was broken and to reassemble them when camp was made (Num. 4:5–15). Moreover, the meaning of עבדה in ch. 18 expands to embrace guard duty as well (n. 277, infra). Thus עבדת מתנה would imply that the total labor of the priesthood in guarding (תשמרו) and removal (ועבדתם) will be rewarded. Interestingly, as Professor S. Lieberman has pointed out to me, Nachmanides, ad loc., converges upon a similar interpretation of מתנה. The possibility must be left open, however—to judge by the readings of the Versions—that ועבדתם may be a gloss. The following words עבדת מתנה אתן את כהנתכם would then be a secondary gloss announcing the priestly gifts in return for their עבדה.

276 For שכר = חלף see Job 10:17b, 14:14b; לשלם חלפת = "to pay a reward" in Phoenician, see "Coronation of Athens," 1.7, H. Donner and W. Rollig, *Kannanäische und Aramäische Inschriften* (1960), 13, n. 60.

277 עבדה cannot be removal labors alone but must include guard duty: (1) The setting is the Tabernacle in camp. (2) Above all, 18:22 is the awaited reply to 17:28, i.e., the people's fear of approaching is now assuaged. (קרב of both passages, of course, refers to the functioning Tabernacle of the settled camp. See § 13.)

278 The translation is incontestable (see the commentaries) but what constitutes the Levitic work here is not clear. It may have been the weighing and recording of the contributions of precious metal, the sums of which immediately follow (vv. 24–29); so

* See n. 277.

† See n. 276.

39:40*b*), an idiom that crops up in Levitic עבדה passages (Num. 4:26, 32[279]). Other indisputable cases are: "So the Israelites had done all the עבדה (work)" (Exod. 39:42)[280] and "Thus was completed all עבדת (the work of) the Tabernacle" (Exod. 39:32).

§ 66. מלאכה. The construct מלאכת עבדה should be rendered "construction project" (Exod. 35:24) and the compound מלאכת עבדת הקדש yields "the project of constructing the sanctuary" or "sanctuary construction project" (Exod. 36:1, 3). A variant of this compound is: "the people bring more than enough for לעשת אתה . . . העבדה למלאכה (the work to carry out the project)" (Exod. 36:5). A different formulation is למלאכת אהל מועד ולכל עבדתו (Exod. 35:21) which translates "for all the construction entailed in the Tent of Meeting project."[281] Since the yet undefined מלאכה is entwined in these and the remaining Tabernacle passage, it becomes imperative to define the term and distinguish it from עבדה.

§ 67. *Its three meanings.* The texts on Tabernacle construction are replete with the use of מלאכה and עבדה. The two are not to be fused or confused but are distinct terminological entities. עבדה reflects the already attested value of physical labor, which in the Tabernacle operation must be rendered as "construction" or "building." However, whereas עבדה is rigidly confined to raw power, מלאכה embraces those tasks where skill exists. The עובד מלאכה and עושה מלאכה approximate the modern distinction of "unskilled laborer," "worker" and "skilled laborer," "artisan." It will be no accident that מלאכה—being a species of work—will exhibit the same Protean range as עבדה. Thus we will have:

(1) the broad general מלאכה, an enterprise calling for skill, workmanship. Menial tasks (עבדה) are, of course, also included in a large enterprise such as the Tabernacle, e.g., raw materials have to be assembled and shipped; manual labor must be available to the artisans. But these are preliminary or ancillary to

---

apparently NJPS. Alternately, it might be rendered "for the work," i.e., for the planks and curtains which became the removal work of the Gershonites and Merarites under Ithamar's supervision (cf. Num. 4:28, 33); so Nachmanides and RSV. However, this second explanation cannot meet the objection that gold was used on all the sacred objects inside the Tabernacle and that the bronze altar is explicitly mentioned (v. 30)— all of which were under Eleazar's charge (Num. 3:32, 4:16). The first answer is therefore preferable.

[279] Num. 4:32*a* should read: "the posts around the enclosure, their sockets, pegs, cords, including all their work tools." לכל כליהם ולכל עבדתם is taken as a hendiadys. The *lamed* coming at the end of a series is conjunctive in force, but stronger than the *waw*, hence "including." See supra n. 237.

[280] See § 67.

[281] Interpreted this way, we have, in effect, a hendiadys of מלאכת עבדה, analogous to the formulation of "work tools" which appears both as כלי עבדה and כלי המשכן בכל עבדתו (Exod. 27:19); see n. 279. The possibility of the following, alternate rendering must not be discounted: "for the craftsmanship of the Tent of Meeting and all its construction work"; מלאכה bearing this second meaning is discussed below.

craftsmanship. Thus, it should be noted that מלאכה is the more general, inclusive term than עבדה, a fact which will be crucial in dealing with מלאכת עבדה later. I therefore render מלאכה as "project" or what the military calls "operation," connoting thereby that the skills of planning and execution direct the physical work.

(2) מלאכה also has a specific meaning—the skill or "craft" employed by each craftsman, e.g., לעשות בכל מלאכת מחשבת "to carry out every craft involving design"; מלאכת חשב, "the designer's craft"; מלאכת חרש "the carver's craft"; and collectively, כל החכמים העשים את כל מלאכת הקדש "all the craftsmen engaged in all the skilled labor of the sanctuary" (Exod. 36:4).[282]

The word עבדה is conspicuously absent in the listing of "all the craftsmen"; indeed in the entire section dealing with Bezalel and his aides, they perform מלאכה, not עבדה (Exod. 35:30–36:8). Moreover, עבדה will never be used whenever any craft is described. There is one ostensible exception, and it supports this rule: "Everyone who would contribute gifts of silver or copper brought them as gifts for the Lord; and everyone who had acacia wood for any of the מלאכת העבדה (construction project) brought that" (Exod. 35:24).[283] Clearly, עבדה is used in connection with wood but not with metal, and it makes sense: the construction of the wooden frames and posts entails heavy, physical labor but silver and copper vessels, sockets, bands, and hooks require workmanship, the skill of artisans.

This distinction between skilled and unskilled labor that underlies מלאכה and עבדה will always be present even when the terms seem synonymous. For example, the completed work of the Tabernacle is called both עבדה and מלאכה (Exod. 39:42f.), but it is noteworthy that it is not its construction work (עבדה) but its artistry[284] (מלאכה) that evokes Moses' blessing. Similarly, the Kohathite role in moving the Tabernacle is called מלאכה as well as עבדה (Num. 4:3f.). We should remember, however, that it is precisely the work of the Kohathites—porterage of the most sacred objects by shoulder—that involved consummate skill: the slightest misstep could lead to direct contact and death (Num. 4:15);[285] the objects under Gershonite and Merarite charge were handled directly and did not require special care.

(3) There is a third meaning to מלאכה found in the Tabernacle texts: the finished product, that which the skill has wrought.[286] Elsewhere in P, this usage approximates the idea of "manufacture," the conversion of raw material into a

---

[282] The craftsmen themselves are also subdivided into עשי מלאכה וחשבי מחשבת "artisans and draftsmen" (Exod. 35:35b), i.e., those who draw up the plans and those who execute them. The latter category would include among others the carver, the embroiderer, and the weaver (Exod. 35:35a).

[283] An alternate translation is possible for לכל מלאכת העבדה: "including all the material for the work." This third meaning of מלאכה is discussed infra. For the use of the *lamed* see supra n. 237 and examples in our text.

[284] Or "the finished product," corresponding to the third meaning of מלאכה discussed below.

[285] See § 33.

[286] E.g., Exod. 22:7, 10; 1 Sam. 15:9; Prov. 24:27; 2 Chron. 17:13.

useful object (e.g., Lev. 7:24, 11:32, 13:51). Since all three meanings of מלאכה are attested in one brief pericope (Exod. 36:1–7), I shall set them side by side with their translations, indicating superlinearly by letters a, b, or c which of the three meanings of מלאכה is manifested. Further interpretation is found in the notes.

§ 68. מלאכה *in Exodus 36:1–7.*

36:1	לעשת את כל מלאכת עבדת הקדש	to carry out the entire construction project[a] of the sanctuary[287]
36:2	לקרבה אל־המלאכה לעשת אתה	to join the project[a] and carry it out[288]
36:3	למלאכת עבדת הקדש לעשת אתה	to carry out the construction project[a] of the sanctuary*
36:4a	העשים את כל־מלאכת הקדש	carrying out all the skilled[b] labor of the sanctuary
36:4b	איש־איש ממלאכתו אשר המה עשים	each from the skilled[b] labor he was carrying out
36:5	מדי העבדה למלאכה...לעשת אתה	enough for the work to carry out the project[a][289]
36:6	אל יעשו עוד מלאכה לתרומת הקדש	make no more material[c] for gifts to the sanctuary[290]
36:7	והמלאכה היתה דים לכל המלאכה לעשות אתה	The material[c] was more than enough to carry out the whole project[a].[291]

Thus, it is clear from the Tabernacle texts that עבדה and מלאכה are two sides of the same semantic coin. They both represent the act of labor, but one

---

[287] How is the double construct מלאכת עבדת הקדש (vv. 1, 3) to be rendered? Alternately one might translate "the skilled[b] labor in the sanctuary construction." However, since the construct מלאכת עבדה is attested but not עבדת הקדש, we must assume that הקדש is affixed to מלאכת עבדה. The term עבדה is explicable in this pericope which deals solely with the Tabernacle craftsmen, because Bezalel and his staff were put in charge of the entire project; they direct the menial labor as well. However, when the commissions of each craftsman is involved, the word עבדה is tellingly missing (Exod. 35:31, 32, 35; 36:2, 4, 4, 8).

[288] Alternately, מלאכה may mean the specific craft: "to participate in the skilled[b] labor and carry it out."

[289] In this verse, the craftsmen act as overseers, reporting that there is enough material (v. 7aα) for all who are employed on the project.

[290] The material required workmanship in advance, even before the craftsmen could utilize it; e.g., the yarn which the women spun (Exod. 35:25); the skins which had to be tanned (v. 23); the acacia logs which had to be sawed into strips (v. 24); and even the gold which had to be refined (found among the people not in ingots but as ornaments, v. 22). Hence מלאכה, implying manufactured goods, is used. This observation is to be credited to Sforno, Nachmanides, and Rashbam, ad loc.

[291] Recognizing that this verse is the duplicate of v. 5 leads to the conjecture that העבדה (v. 5) = והמלאכה (v. 7), and that the writer of v. 5 really meant מדי המלאכה למלאכה "enough material[c] for the project[a]," but to avoid the confusion of two consecutive מלאכה's, he replaced the first with עבדה which we have rendered "more than enough for the work" but where "material" is clearly implied.

*See n. 287.

emphasizes labor that is raw and unskilled, the other trained and skilled. Since both are necessary to any enterprise, they crop up together not only in the Tabernacle construction, but also outside the confines of P wherever construction work is required. Thus, we find מלאכה—עבדה clusters with their distinctions rigorously maintained in accounts of the Temple construction,[292] Temple repairs,[293] construction of the city walls,[294] and others.[295]

§ 69. *Festivals.* The Tabernacle texts offer yet another reason why עבדה must mean "physical labor" and not "service," as so many translators, lexicographers and exegetes[296] have thought. The construct מלאכת עבדה is used twelve times by P in prescribing rest on the festivals.[297] Indeed, if the idiom means "work" in these passages, it should mean the same everywhere in the same

---

[292] Just as the term מלאכה clusters about Bezalel and his fellow artisans, so it makes its appearance in the account of Solomon's Temple only when Hiram is introduced (1 Kings 7:14, 22, 40, 51; 1 Chron. 22:15, 23:4, 28:20f., 29:1, 5; 2 Chron. 4:11, 5:1, 8:16)—another confirmation that מלאכה means (skilled) "work," "craft." (So with Jeroboam, 1 Kings 11:28. In 1 Kings 5:30, 9:23, מלאכה bears the general meaning "project.")

Thus כל מלאכה בנחשת "any work in bronze" (1 Kings 7:14), מלאכת העמודים "the work of the pillars" (ibid., 22); "You have an abundance of המלאכה עשי (craftsmen): stonecutters, masons, carpenters and everyone who is skilled בכל מלאכה (in any craft)" (1 Chron. 22:15).

[293] 2 Kings 12:12, 15, 16, 22:5, 5, 9; 2 Chron. 24:13, 34:10, 12, 13, 17; Hag. 1:14; Ezra 3:8, 9.

[294] E.g., Neh. 4:5, 9, 10, 11, 13, 15, 16, 5:16, 6:3, 9, 16.

[295] E.g., navigation (Ps. 107:23); royal functions (Dan. 8:27; Est. 3:9, 9:3; see Gen. 39:11); husbandry (note the distinction: עשי מלאכת השדה לעבדת האדמה "the farmers who tilled the soil," 1 Chron. 27:26); God's works (Gen. 2:2, 3; Jer. 48:10, 50:25. Isa. 28:21 is no exception [despite S. Daniel, 113]; the use of עבד עבדה for God is to complete the thought of עשה מעשה: "to devise his plan, alien his plan; and to do his work, barbaric his work"; for Isaiah's use of עשה, see 22:11, 32:6, 37:26 ‖ יצר); lifetime "occupation" (Jon. 1:8); or temporary "project," e.g., divorcing foreign wives (Ezra 10:13).

[296] E.g., NJPS, KJV, K-B, עבדה no. 2; C. F. Keil and F. Delitzsch on Exod. 36:1, *The Old Testament*, II (CTL, 1878); a mistake avoided by S. R. Driver (see his Lexicon and Exodus commentary).

[297] Lev. 23:7, 8, 21, 25, 35, 36; Num. 28:18, 25, 26, 29:1, 12, 35. The Sabbath and the Day of Atonement, however, use the phrase כל מלאכה (Lev. 23:3, 28; Num. 29:7; cf. Exod. 31:14f.). This is no accident. For the same distinction exists in regard to the word שבת: the Sabbath and the Day of Atonement alone are described by שבת שבתון (Lev. 23:3, 32; Exod. 16:23, 31:15, 35:2. For the festivals cf. Lev. 23:24, 39, 39). Just as שבת שבתון means "absolute rest" so we must reason that כל מלאכה is severer and more encompassing than מלאכת עבדה. Our knowledge of the austere nature of Sabbath and the Day of Atonement in comparison with the other festivals surely confirms our empirical deductions. Now, however, we have linguistic evidence to buttress our syllogism. For we have discovered in our analysis of the Tabernacle texts that מלאכה is more comprehensive than עבדה: in its meaning "project" (definition 1) it can embrace עבדה. Therefore when כל מלאכה is prohibited on Sabbath and Yom Kippur—days of שבת שבתון

literary source, especially in the context of the Tabernacle construction where, obviously, work is going on!

§ 70. *Census silver.* The last of the eleven instances of עבדה in P, outside the Levitic texts, has heretofore been regarded as a notorious crux: ונתת אתו על עבדת אהל מועד והיה לבני ישראל לזכרון לפני ה' (Exod. 30:16). Indeed, how is it possible for the silver census shekels to become "a service for the Tent" and "a reminder before the Lord"?[298] If, however, we translate: "And assign it for the construction of the Tent[299] . . .," the crux disappears. For we are later told explicitly in the text that this census money was used exclusively for fashioning the silver sockets and decorations of the Tabernacle posts (Exod. 38:25–28). These, standing within the Tabernacle, closed off to the view of the outside world, would, however, physically and visibly be "a reminder before the Lord."[300]

"absolute rest"—every conceivable kind of exertion, skilled and unskilled, heavy or light (physical or mental), is proscribed. Perhaps the best translation of מלאכה would be "activity." The festivals, on the other hand, are bound by מלאכת עבדה, where מלאכה refers to any enterprise or occupation and עבדה is the physical labor attached to it, i.e., "occupational work." Implied perhaps is that light work, unrelated to one's livelihood, would be permitted. We cannot go beyond this tentative suggestion; P's very deliberateness in providing only broad generalizations militates against further specification.

Interestingly enough, P itself provides an alternate description of מלאכת עבדה in the case of the terminal days of the Pesach כל מלאכה לא יעשה בהם אך אשר יאכל לכל נפש הוא לבדו יעשה לכם "no activity should be carried out on them; only what every person is to eat, that alone may be prepared for you" (Exod. 12:16). This would mean that מלאכת עבדה is equivalent to מלאכה with the sole exception of food preparations! (The medieval exegetes, following the rabbinic sages, regard food preparation as an instance of a general principle as, e.g., מלאכת הנאה "pleasure activity" versus necessity [Nach]; מלאכה שלא משתמרת לעבדת קנין "an activity which does not contribute to acquisition," R. Hananel. [Note how this approximates מלאכה as "project."] See esp. Nach on Lev. 23:7; also Ibn Ezra and Rashbam on Exod. 12:16 and Deut. 16:6.) However, this new phraseology produces more problems than it can solve. Are the two P versions (Exod. 12 and Lev. 23, Num. 28) the product of a single ideology (the obvious assumption of rabbinic tradition, see M Beẓ 5:2; M Meg 1:5; B Shab 24*b*, B Pes 47*a*; 83*b*)? Or is the Pesach severer than other festivals in forbidding all activity except food preparation because food prepared before the holiday is liable to be contaminated by leaven?

These, and many additional questions not even raised, bring a halt to an enquiry which demands an essay and not a footnote. Yet enough has been said to illustrate our belief that our newly won understanding of עבדה—מלאכה in P, especially in the Tabernacle texts, casts new light on P's work prohibitions on Sabbaths and Festivals, and the entire question should be reopened.

[298] NJPS and RSV, respectively.

[299] על = "for," "for the purpose of"; see Ehrlich, ad loc. (Heb.).

[300] In my view, it is finally possible to explain why the five pillars at the entrance of the Tent had copper rather than silver sockets (Exod. 26:37, 38:30): simply, being visible from the outside their sanctity was not as great as the other Tabernacle sockets and were disqualified from serving as "a reminder before the Lord."

§ 71. *The paradox.* Thus, I arrive at the conclusion, the ineluctable and paradoxical conclusion, that P, the repository of cultic matters in the Pentateuch, does not use עבדה for cult service, whereas in other Pentateuchal sources this usage is clearly attested.[301] The paradox is intensified by the fact P (and Ezekiel, see anon) never assigns עבדה to the priests,[302] though they are exclusively engaged in the cult service! Its import is realized upon examination of Temple עבדה in indisputably post-exilic texts.

עבדה IN LATER BIBLICAL SOURCES

§ 72. *Chronicles.* Chronicles, in particular, abounds with עבדה and its compounds but reinterprets them and even the Pentateuchal passages in which they occur, so that עבדה-physical labor becomes עבדה-cult service. Thus, כלי עבדה are no longer "work tools"[303] but gilded and silvered "cult vessels" (1 Chron. 28:13–15; cf. 23:26).[304] מלאכת עבדה "building project," under the new interpretation of עבדה, becomes "cultic tasks" of priests (1 Chron. 9:13) or Korahites (1 Chron. 9:19).[305] Above all, all occurrences of the word עבדה in accounts dealing with the Temple seem to refer to cultic service, and the exceptions are easily explicable.[306] Moreover, when it comes to Levitic עבדה the Chronicler describes it in minute detail (1 Chron. 23:26–32; see 9:26–32),[307] thereby giving

---

[301] JE, e.g., noun: Exod. 12:25f., 13:5; verb: Exod. 3:12, 10:26. D, only verb: e.g., Deut. 11:13, 16, 12:2, 30. עבדה with cultic connotations is attributed to a P source once outside the Pentateuch (Josh. 22:27, which more likely is due to the Deuteronomic recension of Joshua) and once in enigmatic Num. 18:7 (see supra n. 275). Indeed, it now turns out that nowhere in the Pentateuch is עבדה ascribed to the functionary whose total preoccupation is with the cultic service, i.e., the priest. For, even in the two above-cited Pentateuchal cases of עבדה, the cultic act is not at the sanctuary! Thus, the severing of the cultic texts of the Pentateuch (and Ezekiel, see anon) from the post-exilic literature is complete.

[302] The only exception is the probably corrupt verse, Num. 18:7 (see n. 275).

[303] E.g., Exod. 27:19; Num. 4:26 (for the Gershonites to uproot the tent stakes). See § 63 and n. 279.

[304] P, in turn, designates cult vessels by כלי השרת (Num. 4:12; see 3:31, 4:9, 14, occurring once in Chronicles, 2 Chron. 24:14) or by the general term כלי הקדש. The verb "to officiate" is expressed in P by שרת, cf. n. 245.

[305] The meaning "physical labor," of course, is not completely supplanted, particularly in the accounts of Temple construction and repair (e.g., 1 Chron. 28:13, 20; 2 Chron. 24:12, 34:13); see the next note.

[306] E.g., 1 Chron. 6:17, 9:13, 23:24, 28–32, 24:3, 25:6; 2 Chron. 8:14, 25:1, 29:35, 31:2, 16, 21, 35:2, 3, 10, 16. The only exceptions are exclusively in the context of Temple construction and repair, and can be explained as being copied by the Chronicler from the older sources before him rather than being his own idiom.

[307] The Chronicler's pro-Levite *Tendenz* is superbly illustrated by comparing 1 Chron. 23:32 with its source in P, Num. 18:3–5. It will be seen at once that the Chronicler has withdrawn משמרת הקדש from the priests and assigned it to the Levites! It may be argued that the Chronicler's basis for his bold rearrangement is in Num.

an accurate picture of the Temple cult of his own day.[308] It seems equally certain that many of the tasks described go back to the first Temple, for with the establishment of a national sanctuary under royal aegis, additional offices were added to the cult apparatus, e.g., singers, musicians, treasurers, inspectors and preparers of sacrificial materials and attendants (all mentioned by Chronicles, supra), not to speak of a bureaucracy to administer them.[309]

§ 73. *Ezekiel's midrash on P.* Is it possible to determine when the change in the meaning of Levitic עבדה took place? Before attempting to answer the question, I call upon the witness of Ezekiel. He is a silent witness but for one verse (44:14), and his silence is eloquent. For, how is it that his Temple vision (chs. 40–48), so replete with descriptions of the worship service and, especially, of the responsibilities of the cultic officials, omits the word עבדה, whereas the Chronicler almost goes out of his way to use עבדה for every feasible aspect of cultic service? There can only be one answer: עבדה in Ezekiel's day did not yet connote what it means in the Chronicler's, and since its Pentateuchal value of Tabernacle removal or construction has obviously no utilitarian value for Ezekiel, he therefore does not resort to it at all.

An argumentum é silencio is precarious; but all suspicions evanesce with examination of its one occurrence (44:14). It is a quotation from P (Num. 18:4a), or rather Ezekiel's recasting of it.[310] The two verses should be compared:

... ושמרו את משמרת אהל מועד לכל עבדת האהל	Num. 18:4a
ונתתי אותם שמרי משמרת הבית לכל עבדתו[311]	Ezek. 44:14
ולכל אשר יעשה בו	

3:28, 32 (W. A. L. Elmslie, *Chronicles* [Cambridge, 1961] ad loc.), but as noted (§ 57 and n. 233), משמרת הקדש is restricted solely to the Kohathites and refers to their guarding duties only *during transit* of the sancta.

That the Chronicler can construct such a far sweeping *midrash halacha* is due to the semantic change that has overtaken both משמרת and עבדה. The Levites in his day, as detailed in this pericope (1 Chron. 23:28ff.), are assisting the priests in the sacrificial service: they prepare the מנחה and the "bread of presence" (v. 29) and are, moreover, responsible for the purity of all the sancta (v. 28). However, only with the new meanings for משמרת and עבדה as "duty" and "cultic service," respectively, does it become possible for the Chronicler to convert his *Tendenz* into legal sanction. (See n. 46 for yet another example.)

[308] For the most recent analysis, see W. Rudolph, *Chronikbücher HAT* (1955) 91 and J. M. Meyers, *Chronicles I* (1965) 72f.

[309] Among additional Levitic officers are: scribes (1 Chron. 24:6; 2 Chron. 34:13), teachers (2 Chron. 17:7–9, 35:3), and fund raisers (2 Chron. 24:5f.).

[310] A variant text is also possible but a written P must nonetheless be postulated.

[311] The switch from לכל עבדת האהל to לכל עבדתו is not capricious but intrinsic to Ezekiel's method. It is based upon משמרת...ו/לכל עבדתו, one of P's idioms for the Levites' duties (Num. 3:25f., 31, 36), and is Ezekiel's way of further strengthening his "Scriptural" support. For the same technique in 44:11b, 14b, see anon.

The import of this borrowing becomes striking upon realization that the verse from Ezekiel concludes and summarizes the Levitic role in the new Temple as detailed three verses earlier (v. 11).

והיו במקדשי משרתים פקדות אל שערי הבית ומשרתים את הבית
המה ישחטו את העולה ואת הזבח לעם והמה יעמדו לפניהם לשרתם

> They shall do guard service in my holy place at the gates of the Temple grounds, and do service in the Temple grounds; they shall slaughter the whole offering and the (well-being) offering for the people, and they shall wait upon them to serve them.

The Levites' first duty is to guard the precinct gates. The text dispatches it in one stich; it is their acknowledged tabernacle function.[312] Their second duty involves "service in the Temple grounds." Elsewhere we learn of a task subsumed under this rubric: to cook the well-being sacrifice for the people (46:24).[313] Ezekiel, however, is not interested in giving us a full definition of Levitic service here. He limits himself to one detail: "they shall slaughter the whole offering and the (well-being) offering for the people," and his reason is clear. It constitutes an innovation, nay—a contradiction. For according to P, the layman alone is responsible for the immolation of the sacrifices he brings (e.g., Lev. 1:5, 11, 3:2, 8, 13, 4:24, 29, 33). Why does Ezekiel deprive the people of their time-honored right? The context gives us the answer: it is not the Levites but the laity who are condemned for allowing foreigners to guard the sancta (vv. 6–8). Indeed, it is Israel who has committed מרי and תועבה and not the Levites! Thus, when Ezekiel transfers ritual slaughter to the Levites he, in effect, punishes the people by barring them from the inner gates where the slaughter takes place (40:39–42). In this regard, the pericope is shown to be in total agreement with Ezekiel's Temple blueprint, for the latter too does not allow the laity to penetrate beyond the outer court. Indeed, this pericope is essential for the innovation, for here and only here is its justification: the house of Israel is punished for its "rebellion," "breaking the covenant,"[314] and "abominations, in admitting foreigners" (vv. 6ff.).[315]

This radical change is even more striking because it is possible to demonstrate that Ezekiel's demand was never carried out. For the Levitic usurpation of

---

[312] That פקדות refers to armed guard service is proven by Ezek. 9:1 (and see 2 Kings 11:18).

[313] משרתי הבית is Ezekiel's appellation for the Levites (45:5) in distinction to the priests who are called משרתי המקדש (45:4).

[314] Read תפרו, LXX.

[315] Ezekiel's midrashic technique is revealing. He states the change and then appends a paraphrase from P (Num. 16:9bβ). Of course, P never bothers to clarify this clause to tell us precisely how Levites shall assist the laity. This is tailor-made for Ezekiel: a perfect opening in which to insert his midrash. For more on his method, see n. 317.

lay slaughter is attributed by the Chronicler to an emergency measure of Hezekiah (2 Chron. 30:17) and a permanent edict of Josiah (2 Chron. 35:6, 11). Even if the Chronicler's allegation concerning this new Levitic prerogative is to be believed and does not reflect an innovation of his own time, it is limited only to the Pesach offering. Furthermore, as is well known, at the end of the second Temple the layman continued to perform the ritual slaughter of his sacrifices (e.g., Jos. *Ant.* III, 9:1; M. Zeb 3:1). Thus, Ezekiel not only differed with P but with subsequent Temple practice.[316]

Now I come to Ezekiel's reinterpretation of עבדה in v. 14. To this paraphrase from P he adds the tell-tale phrase וכל אשר יעשה בו. If עבדה had the general meaning of Levitic service, as found in Chronicles, would Ezekiel have had need for this additional clause? I can only conclude, based on the prophet's refusal to use this word elsewhere, that Ezekiel knew only too well the restricted meaning of עבדה in P, and he therefore found it necessary to gloss his quotation with the explanation that the Levites shall be liable for all labor on the Temple grounds.[317]

---

[316] The historical grounds for Ezekiel's innovation are shrouded in mystery. All that can be said with a modicum of confidence is that there was a movement, undoubtedly initiated by the clergy, to rid the sacrificial court of laymen. The reason, I feel, is most likely religious: the priesthood is charged with the responsibility for the purity of the sancta (so explicitly, Num. 18:1, 5, see §§ 21–24) and the post-exilic priest is expressly warned תשמר את חצרי (Zech. 3:7). (Did, perhaps, the tradition that Solomon had sanctified (קדש) the inner court around the altar give further incentive to ban the זר from it, 1 Kings 8:64?)

We should also reckon with a possible economic motivation: to provide the country Levites with employment in the centralized Temple. If so, then Josiah's reformation is still the decisive historical event behind this pericope, and it cannot be relegated to post-exilic times when there were so few Levites in restored Jerusalem that their tithes were transferred to the priests! Nonetheless, Ezekiel's innovation now turns out to be not as radical as heretofore postulated. For Levitic custody of the Tabernacle is for him a tradition; in effect, he only adds to their duties the sacrificial preparations withdrawn from the laity.

The implications of this interpretation are too vast to be dealt with in this study. It will be readily seen that we have locked horns with a textual beast that has produced much speculation and no little anguish regarding the origins of the Levites. (For the classical position, see J. Wellhausen's *Prolegomena to the History of Ancient Israel* [1957] 121ff. which is founded upon this pericope. For subsequent modifications, see Gunneweg.) Yet, I submit that a study of Ezekiel's midrashic methods will force a re-evaluation of all previously held textual and historical positions. Here, for example, in addition to the demotion of the Levites, now stands unveiled a secondary motive for this pericope—to bar the laity from the inner court. (See supra n. 226; for another example see the next note.)

[317] This is not the place to investigate Ezekiel's midrashic technique. However, I cannot refrain from calling attention to the similar construction of vv. 11 and 14. For just as Num. 16:9bβ was paraphrased to justify the innovation regarding ritual slaughter, another paraphrase of P is utilized to reinterpret עבדה. This catchall addition is וכל אשר יעשה בו and is a recasting of וכל אשר יעשה להם ועבדו (Num. 4:26b). The

Thus, Ezekiel's deliberate abstention from the use of עבדה in general, and his gloss on it when he cites it in a quotation point to the conclusion that עבדה was not the term for the Temple service in Ezekiel's day and that the reinterpretation of P's עבדה, as in Chronicles, was still far off.

§ 74. *Nehemiah's midrash on* עבדה. When did this reinterpretation of Temple עבדה take place? We might surmise it was achieved in the Chronicler's time, were it not for a verse in Nehemiah.[318] It forms part of Nehemiah's covenant: "We lay upon ourselves the obligation to charge ourselves yearly לעבדת (for the cult of) the house of our God: for the Presence bread, the daily cereal offering, the daily whole offering, the . . ." (Neh. 10:33f.). Since עבדה is followed by a list of sacrificial obligations there can be no doubt that cultic service is meant. However, it is the very change in the use of Temple עבדה that enables us to grasp the basis for Nehemiah's innovation. Of a certainty, he has anchored himself on Mosaic precedent: לעבדת בית אלהינו of Nehemiah is clearly על עבדת אהל מועד of Exodus 30:16, but the meaning is no longer the same. As we have observed (§ 70), the shekels of Exodus' one-time census were devoted to the one-time construction (עבדה) of the Tabernacle (see Exod. 30:16 and 38:25–28) and have nothing to do with an annual tax.[319]

Resort to the Tabernacle precedent is later attested for King Joash (2 Chron. 24:4–14) who imposes "the Mosaic tax" (משאת משה) for repairing the Temple in his day. Since Joash collects his tax *yearly*—until the repairs are completed[320]— it forms an intermediate stage to the development of Nehemiah's tax. But Joash has introduced no innovation; his עבדה still means "construction" work in a strict sense. Nehemiah, however, breaks away from this semantic restriction by his use of עבדה as "cult service." The needs of עבדה-cult, being perpetual, can

---

latter has its textual problems, but it clearly means one of two things: the LXX apparently reads בהם in which case it refers to the כלי עבדה, "the work tools" (see n. 303) or Ms. להם is correct and refers to the courtyard curtains. (It should be noted that Ezekiel refrains from citing the final ועבדו, though had it connoted "service" it would have suited his purpose perfectly!)

[318] עבדה occurs also once in Ezra, 8:20, where it clearly refers to physical labor.

[319] G. Beer and K. Galling, *Exodus* (1939) ad loc., hold that the Mosaic impost was also annual, followed by W. Rudolph, *Esra-Nehemiah, HAT* (1949) 177–179. This is also the rabbinic viewpoint (e.g., Y Shek 4*b*) and is upheld by Josephus (*Ant.* IX, 8:2).

[320] So we must conclude; see the cogent argumentation of Kaufmann, *Toledot* IV (1956) 333, n. 46 (Heb.). Joash's משאת may, however, refer to the Mosaic תרומה, the proceeds of the Tabernacle building fund campaign (Exod. 25) rather than to the census money, so Kaufmann, loc. cit., followed by J. Liver, "The Ransom" 57–59, n. 3. The latter adds a philological argument that the meaning of משאת is more likely "contribution" (Ezek. 20:40 and Phoenician) rather than an alleged hapax derived from נשא ראש (Exod. 30:12) meaning "tax." If correct, then this intermediary step in the evolution of Nehemiah's midrash would be eliminated.

only be requited through a yearly tax. Thus Nehemiah's edict is without precedent but it is not arbitrary. It is Scripture reinterpreted; it is midrash.[321]

§ 75. *Recapitulation and conclusion.* עבדה meaning cult service is found in all Pentateuchal sources but P, and predominantly in post-exilic historical texts. P's עבדה, on the other hand, is confined to "physical labor" and, in the special case of the Levites, to their Tabernacle function as sacred furniture movers. Moreover, there is no intimation anywhere in P either of the post-exilic use of עבדה for "Temple cult" in general, or of the post-exilic Levitic עבדה as Temple singers, administrators and cult assistants, in particular. The cultic backgrounds of Chronicles and P are worlds apart.[322] These facts lead to but one conclusion: the עבדה passages in P are old, pre-exilic materials which were allowed to experience reinterpretation but no inner editorial change.[323] Thus the case of the Levitic עבדה and its reflexes in the Bible can be added to the fast-growing portfolio on behalf of the antiquity of the materials comprising the Priestly source.[324]

---

[321] Only now can it be seen as cut of the same cloth as the rest of Nehemiah's covenant (see *Toledot*, 331–338). As for the different shekel weights, the most plausible answer is that the one-third Persian shekel was Nehemiah's calculated equivalent to the Pentateuch's half shekel (so Nachmanides on Exod. 30:12). See Rudolph, op. cit., supra n. 319, for references and J. N. Epstein, *Introduction to Tannaitic Literature* (1957) 337 (Heb.), and H. Albeck, introduction to M Sheḳ, P. 184, for rabbinic precedents. J. Liver, ibid., asserts that Nehemiah's edict could not be based on Exodus because, in rabbinic times, the term half shekel was used even when the currency changed; the Rabbis, then, not Nehemiah, worked a midrash. However, Liver, himself, has argued persuasively that the annual Temple tax was a rabbinic, post-Hasmonean innovation and Nehemiah's edict, at best, had a short life. Thus, he may no longer use rabbinic procedure anachronistically as a standard for Nehemiah. Since the Rabbis and Nehemiah are both innovators, each is entitled to develop his midrash by his own criteria.

[322] As observed (nn. 305f.), עבדה in Chronicles retains the meaning of physical labor relating to the Sanctuary only in quotations from P, but otherwise in the cult means "Temple service." The final stage in the history of this term takes us into rabbinical literature where all forms of the root are assiduously avoided in describing any physical labor done in the Temple. Full documentation cannot be adduced here, but for a characteristic example, see Tosef Kel B.K. 1:11 and its discussion in Erub 105*a*.

[323] Precluded from this conclusion, of course, is the work of the redactor, i.e., the selection and arrangement of the material, the composition of frameworks and transitions.

[324] See Kaufmann, *Toledot*, I, 113ff. (Heb.) [Greenberg abridg.-trans., 175–199], and a summary of Kaufmann's position in M. Greenberg, "A New Approach to the History of the Israelite Priesthood," *JAOS* (1950) 70:41–47. Also see E. A. Speiser, "Leviticus and the Critics," *Kaufmann Jubilee Volume* (1960) 29–49; and for the Tabernacle texts in particular, see F. M. Cross, 52–54 (= *BA Reader*, I, 209–212); A. Hurvitz, "The Usage of שש and בוץ in the Bible and its Implication for the Date of P,' *HTR* (1967) 60:117–121; Haran, *Scripta*, §§ 21ff.; and J. A. Scott.

INDICES

BIBLIOGRAPHY

BIBLICAL

The Hebrew Scriptures. R. Kittel's *Biblia Hebraica*, ed.[4] Edited by A. Alt and O. E. Eissfeldt, 1937.
The Septuagint. Edited by H. B. Swete, 1887–1894.
The Targums. In *Miqraot Gedolot*, 1912, often reprinted.

HELLENISTIC

Works of Philo. ("Loeb Classics")
Works of Josephus. ("Loeb Classics")

ANCIENT NEAR EAST

Ancient Near Eastern Texts, ed.[2] Edited by J. Pritchard, 1955.

RABBINIC

Mishna. Vilna edition, frequently reprinted.
Tosefta, ed.[2] Edited by M. S. Zuckermandel, 1938.
Babylonian Talmud. Vilna edition, frequently reprinted.
Jerusalem Talmud. Most recent edition, 1959.
Mekilta of Rabbi Simeon. Edited by Hoffmann, 1905.
Sifra. Edited by Weiss, 1862.
Sifre, Numbers. Edited by Horovitz, 1917.
Sifre Zuta. Edited by Horovitz, Supplement to *Sifre*, Numbers, cited above.
Midrash Rabba. Vilna edition, frequently reprinted.
Midrash Tanhuma. Vilna edition, frequently reprinted.
Yalkut Shimoni. Vilna edition, frequently reprinted.

MEDIEVAL HEBREW COMMENTARIES ON THE TORAH

Rashi, Rashbam, Abraham Ibn Ezra, Nachmanides (Ramban), Kli Yaqar, found in *Miqraot Gedolot*.
    Vienna, 1859, often reprinted.
Abarbanel. Jerusalem, 1964, 3 vols.
Bechor Shor. Edited by J. Gad, Jerusalem, 1956–1960, 3 vols.

MODERN TRANSLATIONS OF THE HEBREW SCRIPTURES

The Torah—A New Translation. Jewish Publication Society, 1962.
Revised Standard Version, 1952.
Le sainte Bible. Leviticus, 1958; Numbers, 1958. Edited by H. Cazelle.
Jewish Publication Society, 1917.
King James Version, 1611.

COMMENTARIES AND STUDIES

Aharoni, Y. "Arad: Its Inscriptions and Temple," *BA* (1968) 31:2–32.
Albeck, Y., and H. Yalon. *Commentary on the Mishna.* 1957–1959, 6 vols. (Heb.).
Albright, W. F. *Archaeology and the Religion of Israel.* 1942.
The Assyrian Dictionary. Chicago, 1964-, 9 vols. to date.
Bartinoro, R. Obadiah of. *Commentary on the Mishna.* Warsaw, ed. 1884, often reprinted.
Beer, G., and K. Galling. *Exodus.* 1939.

Bickerman, E. J. "The Warning Inscription of Herod's Temple," *JQR* (1946–1947) 37:387–405.

———. "Une proclamation Sélucide relative an temple de Jérusalem," *Syria* (1947) 25:69–85.

Brown, F., S. R. Driver, and C. A. Briggs. *Hebrew and English Lexicon of the Old Testament*. 1957.

Caplice, R. "Namburbi Texts in the British Museum," *Orientalia* (1965) 34:105–131; (1967) 36:1–38, 273–298.

Cassuto, U. *A Commentary on the Book of Genesis*. Part II, *From Noah to Abraham*. 1964.

Cooke, G. A. *Ezekiel*, ICC. 1936.

Cross, F. M. "The Priestly Tabernacle," *BA* (1947) 10:45–68 (reprinted in *The Biblical Archaeologist Reader*, I, 201–228).

Cross, F. M., and D. N. Freedman. "The Blessing of Moses," *JBL* (1948) 67:191–210.

Daniel, S. *Recherches sur le vocabularie du culte dans le Septante*. 1966.

Daube, D. *Studies in Biblical Law*. 1947.

Davies, H. "The Ark of the Covenant," *ASTI* (1966–1967) 5:30–47.

Donner, H., and W. Rollig. *Kanaanäische und aramäische Inschriften*. 1960.

Driver, G. R. "Three Technical Terms in the Pentateuch," *JSS* (1956) 1:97–105.

Driver, S. R. *Deuteronomy*, ICC. 1895.

———. *Exodus*. Cambridge, 1911.

———. *Notes on the Hebrew Text of the Books of Samuel*. 2nd ed., 1913.

Eerdmans, B. P. "The Composition of Numbers," *OTS* (1949) 6:101–216.

Ehrlich, A. B. *Hamiqra Kifshuto*. 1901. 3 vols. (Heb.).

———. *Randglossen zur hebräischen Bibel*. 1908–1914. 7 vols.

Eissfeldt, O. *Das Lied Moses*, BAL. 1958.

———. *The Old Testament: An Introduction*. Translated by P. R. Ackroyd, 1965.

Elliger, K. *Leviticus*, HAT. 1966.

Elmslie, W. A. L. *Chronicles*. Cambridge, 1916.

Epstein, J. N. *Introduction to Tannaitic Literature*. 1957 (Heb.).

Frankfort, H. *The Art and Architecture of the Ancient Orient*. 1954.

Fretheim, T. E. "The Priestly Document: Anti-Temple?", *VT* (1968) 18:313–329.

Friedrich, J. *Die hethitischen Gesetze*. 1959.

———. *Hethitisches Wörterbuch*. 1952.

Gese, H. *Der Verfassungsentwurf des Ezechiel, Kap. 40–48*, BHTh. 1957.

Gesenius, F. H. W., and F. Buhl. *Hebräisches und aramäisches Handwörterbuch*. 1910.

———, E. Kautzsch, and A. E. Cowley. *Gesenius' Hebrew Grammar*. Eng. ed.[2] 1910.

Goetze, A. "Instructions for Temple Officials," *ANET*, ed.[2] 1955. Pp. 207–210.

———. "On the Hittite Words for 'Year' and the Seasons and for 'Night' and 'Day,'" *Language* (1951) 27:467–476.

———. Review of E. von Schuler, *Hethitische Dienstanweisungen*, *JCS* (1959) 13:65–70.

Gordon, C. H. *Ugaritic Textbook*. 1965.

Gray, G. B. *Numbers*, ICC. 1903.

Gray, J. *The Book of Kings*, OTL. 1963.

Greenberg, M. "A New Approach to the History of the Israelite Priesthood," *JAOS* (1950) 70:41–47.

———. "Crimes and Punishments," *IDB*, I. 1962. Pp. 733–744.

———. "Some Postulates of Biblical Criminal Law," *Y. Kaufmann Jubilee Volume*. Edited by M. Haran, 1960. Pp. 5–28.

Greenstone, J. H. *Numbers*. 1939.

Gunneweg, A. H. J. *Leviten und Priester*, FRLANT. 1965.

Gurney, O. R. *The Hittites*. 1952.

Güterbock, H. G. "Wachbezirk," *JCS* (1952) 6:35f.

Haran, M. "The Complex of Ritual Acts Performed Inside the Tabernacle," *Scripta Hiersolymitana*, VIII (1961). Edited by C. Rabin. Pp. 272–302.

———. "The Disappearance of the Ark," *IEJ* (1963) 13:46–57.

———. *Between* Ri'shonōt *and* Ḥadashōt. 1963 (Heb.).

———. "The Graded Taboos of Holiness," *Sefer Segal*. 1965. Pp. 33–41 (Heb.).

———, editor. *Y. Kaufmann Jubilee Volume*. 1960.

———. "Priesthood," *Ency. Miq.*, IV. 1962. Cols. 14–45 (Heb.).

———. "The Priestly Image of the Tabernacle," *HUCA* (1965) 36:191–226.

Haran, M. "Shilo and Jerusalem," *JBL* (1962) 81:14–24.

Hillers, D. R. "Ritual Procession of the Ark and Ps. 132," *CBQ* (1968) 30:48–55.

Hurvitz, A. "The Usage of שש and בץ in the Bible and its Implication for the Date of P," *HTR* (1967) 60:117–121.

Imparati, F. *Le leggi Ittite.* 1964.

Interpreter's Dictionary of the Bible. 1962. 4 vols.

Japhet, S. "The Supposed Common Authorship of Chronicles and Ezra-Nehemia Investigated Anew," *VT* (1968) 18:330–371.

Jean, C. F., and J. Hoftijzer. *Dictionnaire des inscriptions sémitiques.* 1965.

Joint Expedition with the Iraq Museum at Nuzi.

Joüon, P. *Grammaire de l'Hébreu Biblique.* 1965.

Junker, H. "Vorschriften fur den Tempelkult in Philä," *Analecta Biblica* (1959) 12:151–160.

Kaufmann, Y. *Judges.* 1962 (Heb.).

———. *Toledot ha-Emuna ha-Yisraelit.* 1938–1956; 4 vols. abridged and translated by M. Greenberg, *The Religion of Israel,* 1960.

Keil, C. F., and F. Delitzsch. *The Old Testament* II, CTL. 1878.

Kilmer, A. Draffkorn. "Ilāni/Elohim," *JBL* (1957) 76:216–224.

Koch, K. "Der Spruch 'Sein Blut bleibe auf seinem Haupt'" *VT* (1962) 12:396–416.

Köhler, L., and W. Baumgartner. *Lexicon in Veteris Testamenti Libros.* 1951, 1953. 2 vols.

Krause, K. "Boğasköy Tempel V," *Instanbular Forschungen,* XI. 1940.

de Leon, Isaac. *Megillat Esther,* A Rebuttal to Nachmanides' Critique of Maimonides' *Sefer ha-Mitzvot.* In *Sefer Machshevet Moshe.* 1866, and reprinted separately.

Lambert, W. G. "Literary Style in First Millenium Mesopotamia," *JAOS* (1968) 88:123–132.

Levine, B. "Notes on a Number of Technical Terms of the Biblical Cult," *Leshonenu* (1965) 30:2–11 (Heb.).

Licht, J. S. "Levi," *Ency. Miq.,* IV. 1962. Cols. 467–472 (Heb.).

Liver, J. "Korah, Dathan and Abiram," *Scripta Hierosolymitana,* VIII. 1961. Pp. 189–217.

———. "The Ransom of the Half Shekel," *Y. Kaufmann Jubilee Volume.* 1960. Pp. 54–67 (Heb.).

Loewenstamm, S. E. "*Kārēt,*" *Ency. Miq.* IV. 1962. Cols. 330–332 (Heb.).

McNeile, A. M. *Numbers.* Cambridge, 1931.

Maimonides. *The Code (Mishne Torah).* 1947. 5 vols. (Heb.).

———. *Sefer ha-Mitzvot.* Contained in *Sefer Machshevet Moshe,* 1866, and reprinted often separately.

Meyers, J. M. *Chronicles.* Anchor, 1965. 2 vols.

Möhlenbrink, K. "Die levitischen Überlieferungen des Alten Testaments," *ZAW* (1934) 52, N.F. 11:184–231.

Montgomery, J., and H. Gehman. *Kings,* ICC. 1951.

Moraldi, L. *Espiazione sacrificiali e riti espiatori nell'ambiente biblico e nell'Antico Testamento.* 1956.

Muilenburg, J. *Isaiah: Chs. 40–66.* Interpreter's Bible, V. 1956.

Nachmanides. Critique of Maimonides' *Sefer ha-Mitzvot.* In *Sefer Machshevet Moshe.* 1866, and reprinted separately.

Neufeld, E. *The Hittite Laws.* 1951.

Noth, M. *Exodus.* Translated by J. S. Bowden, OTL. 1962.

———. "David and Israel, in II Sam. 7," *The Laws in the Pentateuch and Other Studies.* 1966. Pp. 250–259. (Translated by Ap-Thomas; reprinted from *Mélanges Bibliques rédigés en l'honneur de André Robert,* 1957, pp. 122–130.)

———. "Jerusalem and the Israelite Tradition," ibid. Pp. 132–144. (Translated by Ap-Thomas; reprinted from *OTS,* 1950, 8:28–46.)

———. *The History of Israel.* 1958.

Nougayrol, J. *Ugaritica V,* Mission de Ras Shamra, ed. C. F. A. Schaeffer. 1968.

Pedersen, J. *Israel: Its Life and Culture.* 1940. 4 vols. (2 books).

Philo. *Moses.* (Loeb VI)

———. *On Rewards and Punishment.* (Loeb VIII)

Raban, N. "The Entrance to the Tent of Meeting," *Tarbiz* (1951) 23:1–8 (Heb.).

Rabe, V. W. "The Temple as Tabernacle." Harvard Univ. dissertation. 1963.

von Rad, G. *Die Priesterschrift im Hexateuch.* Literarisch untersucht und theologisch gewertet *BWANT,* 65. 1934.

Reiner, E. "Lipšur Litanies," *JNES* (1956) 15:129–149.

————. "La Magie babylonienne," *Le monde du sorcier* (Sources orientales, 7). 1966. Pp. 69–98.

Ritter, E. K. "Magical-Expert and Physician," *Assyriological Studies* (Landsberger vol.) XVI. 1965.

Rowley, H. H. *Worship in Ancient Israel*. 1967.

Rudolph, W. *Chronikbücher, HAT*. 1955.

————. *Esra-Nehemiah, HAT*. 1949.

Samson of Sens. *Commentary on the Mishna*. Vilna ed., 1912, often reprinted.

von Schuler, E. *Hethitische Dienstanweisungen*. 1957.

————. "Hethitische Kultbräuche in dem Brief eines ugaritischen Gesandten," *RHA* (1953) 72:43–46.

Scott, J. A. "The Pattern of the Tabernacle." Univ. of Pennsylvania dissertation on microfilm. 1965.

Snijders, L. A. "The Meaning of *zar* in the Old Testament," *OTS* (1954) 10:1–154.

Speiser, E. A. "Leviticus and the Critics," *Y. Kaufmann Jubilee Volume*. Edited by M. Haran, Jerusalem, 1960. Pp. 29–45 [= *Oriental and Biblical Studies*, edited by J. Finkelstein and M. Greenberg (1967), pp. 123–142].

————. "Unrecognized Dedication," *IEJ* (1963) 13:69–73.

————. "The Durative Hithpa'el: a *tan*-Form," *JAOS* (1955) 75:52–55 [= *Oriental and Biblical Studies*, edited by J. J. Finkelstein and M. Greenberg (1967), pp. 506–514].

Sturtevant, E. H., and G. Bechtel. *A Hittite Chrestomathy*. 1935.

Thompson, R. C. *Assyrian Medical Texts*. 1923.

Tsevat, M. "Studies in the Book of Samuel," I, *HUCA* (1961) 31:191–216.

Ussishkin, D. "Building IV in Hamath and the Temples of Solomon and Tell Tayanat" *IEJ* (1966) 16:104–110.

de Vaux, R. *Ancient Israel*. Translated by J. McHugh, 1961.

————. "Arche d'Alliance et Tente de Réunion," *Memorial A. Gelin*. 1961. Pp. 55–70.

Vieyra, M. "Le sorcier hittite," *Le monde du sorcier* (Sources orientales, 7). 1966. Pp. 101–125.

Vincent, A. "Les rites du balancement (tenoûphâh) et du prélèvement (teroûmâh) dans le sacrifice de communion de l'Ancien Testament," *Mélanges Syriens offerts à R. Dussaud*, I. 1939. Pp. 267–272.

Wachter, T. *Reinheitsvorschriften im griechischen Kult*. 1910.

Wellhausen, J. *Prolegomona to the History of Ancient Israel*. (English translation, Meridian paperback, 1957.)

de Wit, C. "Les inscriptions des lions-gargouilles du temple d'Edfou," *Chronique d'Égypte* (1954) 57:29–45.

Wright, G. E. "The Controversy of God: A Form-Critical Study of Deuteronomy 32," *Essays Muilenburg*. 1962. Pp. 26–27.

Zimmerli, W. *Ezechiel*, BK, 13. 1959, fasc. 6; 1967, fasc. 13–14.

————. "Die Eigenart der prophetischen Rede des Ezechiel," *ZAW* (1954) 66:1–26.

ABBREVIATIONS NOT EXPLAINED IN TEXT

AMT	*Assyrian Medical Texts*	*HC*	*A Hittite Chrestomathy*, Sturtevant and Bechtel
ANET	*Ancient Near Eastern Texts*, Edited by J. Pritchard	*HG*	*Die hethitischen Gesetze* (1959), J. Friedrich
ASTI	*Annual of the Swedish Theological Institute in Jerusalem*, Leiden	*HL*	*The Hittite Laws* (1951), E. Neufeld
AT	American Translation (of the Old Testament, 1931)	*HTR*	*Harvard Theological Review*
		HUCA	*Hebrew Union College Annual*
B	Babylonian	ICC	International Critical Commentary
b	ben	*IDB*	*Interpreter's Dictionary of the Bible*
BA	*The Biblical Archaeologist*	*IEJ*	*Israel Exploration Journal*
BAL	*Berichte über der Verhandlungen der Sächsischen Akademie der Wissenschaften zu Leipzig*	J	Yahwist source
		JAOS	*Journal of the American Oriental Society*
B-D-B	Brown-Driver-Briggs, *Hebrew and English Lexicon of the Old Testament*	*JBL*	*Journal of Biblical Literature*
		JCS	*Journal of Cuneiform Studies*
Bek	Bekorot	JE	Yahwist-Elohist source
ber.	beraita	JEN	Joint Expedition with the Iraq Museum at Nuzi
Beẓ	Beẓa	JPS	Jewish Publication Society
BH	Biblia Hebraica, ed.[4]	*JQR*	*Jewish Quarterly Review*
BHTh	*Beiträge zur historischen Theologie*	*JSS*	*Journal of Semitic Studies*
BK	*Biblischer Kommentar Altes Testament*	K-B	Köhler-Baumgartner, *Lexicon in Veteris Testamenti Libros*, 2 vols.
B.K.	Baba Ḳama	Kel	Kelim
B.M.	Baba Meẓi'a	KJV	King James Version (1611)
BWANT	*Beitrage zur Wissenschaft vom Alten und Neuen Testament*	*LI*	*Le Leggi Ittite*, F. Imparati (1964)
		LXX	Septuagint
CAD	*The Assyrian Dictionary*, Chicago	M	Mishna
CBQ	*The Catholic Biblical Quarterly*	Mek	Mekilta
CTL	Clark's Theological Library	Meg	Megilla
D	Deuteronomic source	Mid	Middot
DISO	*Dictionnaire des inscriptions sémitiques de l'ouest*	Nach	Nachmanides
		Ned	Nedaba
E	Elohist source	Neg	Nega'im
Ency. Miq.	*Encyclopedia Miqrait*, 5 vols. (Heb.)	NJPS	The Torah—*A New Translation*, Jewish Publication Society
FRLANT	*Forschungen zur Religion und Literatur des Alten und Neuen Testaments*	*OTL*	*The Old Testament Library*
		OTS	*Oudtestamentische Studien*
		P	Priestly source
G-B	Gesenius-Buhl, *Hebräisches und aramäisches Handwörterbuch*	Par	Parasha
		Pes	Pesaḥim
G-K-C	Gesenius-Kautzsch-Cowley, *Hebrew Grammar*	R	Rabbi, Rabba
HAT	*Handbuch zum Alten Testament*	*RA*	*Revue d'Assyriologie et d'archiologie Orientale*

RHA	*Revue Hittite et Asianique*	Tam	Tamid
RSV	Revised Standard Version (1953)	Tanḥ	Tanḥuma
Sanh	Sanhedrin	TJ	Targum, Pseudo-Jonathan
SB	Le Sainte Bible	Tosef	Tosefta
Scripta	*Scripta Hierosolymitana*, VIII	*VT*	*Vetus Testamentum*
Shab	Shabbat	Y	Yerushalmi (Jerusalemite)
Shebu	Shebu'ot	*ZAW*	*Zeitschrift für die Alttestamentliche*
Sheḳ	Sheḳalim		*Wissenschaft*
Suk	Sukka	Zeb	Zebaḥim
SVT	*Supplements to Vetus Testamentum*		

TERMS DISCUSSED

Boldface numbers refer to sections in text; all other numbers refer to footnotes.

HEBREW

אל פני/ את פני	146, 154
את = עם = על = לפני	201
בא‖ ראה‖ גלה	127
בא/ שב	265
בין האולם למזבח	166
בית מקדש	48, 78
היה למשמרת	**6**
היכל/ בית	47
הקרב אל/ על/לפני	140
התהלך	249f.
והם ישאו עונם	**20–26**
זר	6
חלף/שכר	276
יומת	**17, 24, 41**
ימות	**2, 19**, 26, 76
כלי מלאכה	297
כלי עבדה	279, 281, 303
כלי קדש	186
כ˙פר	**28f.**
כפר	**27–30**
כפרה	115
לזכרון	**70**
לכל/וכל	237, 262, 279
לקח	246
מבית	251
מדי העבדה למלאכה	291
מלאכה	**66–68**
מלאכת עבדה	**66–69**, 72
מלאכת עבדת הקדש	**68**
מקדש	78
משא	**56–60**

משאת	319
משכנת	251
משמרת ה'	**6**
משמרת משא	**57**
נגע	128, 173
נגש/ קרב	**31–34, 39**, 217
נתן	257
נתן/ מתנה	103, **64**, 275
עבדה	**52–75**
עבדת מתנה	275
עבדת עבדה	**56**
על	299
על פי ה'	37
עמד לפני	201
עשה‖ יצר	295
פולחן	243
פקדות	311
פתח אהל מועד	**12**
צבא	**54**
קדש	149, 182
קדש קדשים	Intro.; **16**, 72, 162, 211
קצף/ נגף	**17**, 75, 109
קרב	**31–41**, 130
ראש	239
שבת שבתון	297
שמר משמרת	**17–19**, 24, **29f., 44, 47, 54**, 41, 44
שמר הסף	197
שרת	245
תנופה	101f.

97

SEPTUAGINT

’αναφορά   **60**
λειτουργία   243
ἔργον   243

AKKADIAN

batqa ṣabātu	51	maṣṣartu	203
ṭeḫû	133	nazāzu	206
qrb	**35**		

HITTITE

ᴸᵁḫaliyattalla	192, 194	araḫzenaš	205
araḫza ḫali	191	ᴸᵁUBĀRU	205
ᴸᵁweḫiškattalleš	194	tiyazi	206
ḫali	203		

REFERENCES

Boldface numbers refer to sections in text; all other numbers refer to footnotes.

BIBLICAL SOURCES

Genesis
2:2, 3............................295
3:8.............................250
4:9..............................29
9:22............................127
20:4............................127
30:28f..........................246
 :31.............................29
32:21...........................114
34...............................**45**
 :31.............................10
39:11...........................295
40:3f............................28
42:17, 19........................28
49:5–7..........................**45**

Exodus
3:5............................141
 :12...........................301
10:26..........................301
12.............................297
 :5.............................51
 :6...........................**6**;59
 :16.......................297(2×)
 :25f..........................301
 :48............................32
13:5...........................301
 :21...........................170
14:20..........................121
16:23...........................51
 :31...........................297
19.............................**42**
 :1, 2a........................167
 :9............................**43**
 :10f..........................**43**
 :12.............................**2**
 :12b..........................**43**
 :13........................**42**;16
 :14f..........................**43**
 :15...........................127

Exodus (cont.)
19:16..........................**43**
 :20...........................**43**
 :20b..........................**43**
 :21........................**42, 43**
 :21b.......................**43**(2×)
 :22...........................**42**
 :22b..........................**43**
 :24...........................**42**
 :24b.......................**43**(2×)
20:5...........................219
 :21b..........................254
 :26...........................149
21:17...........................13
 :30...........................112
22:1............................10
 :6.............................29
 :7............................286
 :10...........................286
24:1.......................**43**, 172
 :4........................**43**(2×)
 :5............................172
 :10...........................172
 :13...........................**43**
 :15f..........................**43**
 :17........................169, 170
25.........................168, 320
 :8.............................78
 :22...........................**42**
 :35...........................154
26:37..........................300
27:19......................281, 303
 :19a..........................**65**
 :21...........................154
28f............................172
 :1.....................123, 125, 141
 :29...........................149
 :35............**37, 38**;18, 149
 :43..........**2, 37, 39**;148, 165
29..........................46, 103

Exodus (cont.)

29:4.........................141
  :9a........................148
  :21........................124
  :29........................102
  :33......................6, 106
  :37........................128
  :38........................141
30:4........................154
  :6.........................154
  :12.............28; 75, 239(2×), 321
  :14f.......................297
  :15.........................28
  :16..........28(2×), 70, 74; 108, 109
  :20.......................39, 18
  :20f......................2, 37
  :26a........................72
  :26–28.....................124
  :26–29......................40
  :26–30.....................211
  :29.....................72, 128
  :29b.......................124
  :30........................124
  :33.........................6
31:14f.......................2
  :15........................297
32..........................187
  :17.........................43
  :25–29......................45
  :27–29.....................185
  :35........................109
33:5b–7......................252
  :9f........................169
  :11........................245
34:2b........................43
35:2......................2; 297
  :9.........................149
  :21.........................66
  :22........................290
  :23........................290
  :24.................66, 67; 209
  :25........................290
  :30–36:8....................67
  :31........................287
  :32........................287
  :35........................287
  :35a.......................282
  :35b.......................282
36:1.....................66; 287
  :1–7....................67, 68
  :2.........................287
  :3.....................66; 287
  :4................67; 287(2×)
  :5.....................66; 291
  :7....................291, 292
  :7a........................289

Exodus (cont.)

36:8........................287
  :11........................296
  :22........................292
38:21.......................65
  :24–29.....................278
  :25–28..................70, 74
  :30...................278, 300
39:1........................149
  :32.........................65
  :40.........................65
40:2........................141
  :9.........................72
  :9–16......................211
  :19........................249
  :32.........................37
  :34........................169
  :38........................169

Leviticus

1...........................165
  :1.........................111
  :3.........................141
  :3–6........................12
  :4.........................104
  :5.................73; 141, 226
  :6.........................226
  :9.........................226
  :11.........................73
  :15........................141
  :28........................141
2:8.....................141(2×)
3:2....................73; 104
  :8.........................73
  :9.........................141
  :13........................73
4:5–7.......................150
  :6.........................146
  :10........................141
  :15........................104
  :16–18.....................150
  :17........................146
  :24........................104
  :29....................73; 104
  :33.........................73
5:1.........................95
  :2.........................162
  :14.........................88
6:3........................149
  :6.........................141
  :7.........................141
  :11........................128
  :20........................128
  :23........................150
7:8........................141
  :24.........................67

Leviticus (cont.)

8.........................46, 103, 172
  :3f..............................**12**
  :22.............................102
  :30..............................35
  :35.......................**6**; 35(2×)
9:4f..............................**43**
  :5..............................**12**
  :6...............................**2**
  :8.............................141
  :9........................**2**; 141
  :23f............................169
  :24.............................**43**
10...............................17
  :6.............................145
  :7.............................157
  :9........................**37**; 18
  :10...........................**a**; 1
  :17............................149
  :18............................149
11:32.............................**67**
12:4.........................78, 211
13:36.............................51
  :51.............................**67**
14:13............................149
  :57...........................**a**; 1
15:16f...........................152
  :31...........................**a**; 1
16..............................211
  :1f..............................17
  :2.......................**2, 43**; 76
  :2ff.............................**43**
  :3ff.............................17
  :4.............................150
  :5.............................141
  :9.............................141
  :13..............................**2**
  :17............................150
  :24............................165
  :33..............................78
17:16.............................95
18.........................10, 127
  :6..........................127(2×)
  :7–19..........................127
  :14.........................127(2×)
  :19............................127
  :20............................119
  :28............................119
  :29..............................10
  :30...............................6
19:20..............................**2**
  :30..............................78
20.......................13, 25, 127
  :1–5.............................**51**
  :2.........................**2**; 11
  :3..............................78

Leviticus (cont.)

20:9...............................**2**
  :9–16............................10
  :10...............................**2**
  :11...........................**2**; 10
  :12...........................**2**; 10
  :13...........................**2**; 10
  :14............................246
  :15...............................**2**
  :16.....................**2**; 10, 127
  :17............95, 127(2×), 246
  :17–19...........................10
  :18............................127
  :19.............................95
  :20.............................95
  :20–21...........................10
  :21............................246
  :27..............................**2**
21:2..............................19
  :7*b*............................153
  :10.............................19
  :10–15...........................**38**
  :12.............................78
  :13............................246
  :14............................246
  :16–23.......................**38**(2×)
  :17...................**37, 39**; 158
  :18.............................**37**
  :21...................**37, 398**; 51
  :22.............................**38**
  :23...............**37**; 78, 154, 158
  :23*a*.....................**47**; 158
22:3........................120, 140
  :3*b*............................140
  :3–9.............................20
  :9.............**2, 6**; 20, 91, 140, 143
  :10–12............................6
  :13............................140
  :22..........................141(2×)
23..............................297
  :3...........................297(2×)
  :7...........................297(2×)
  :8...........................297(2×)
  :21............................297
  :24............................297
  :25............................297
  :28............................297
  :32............................297
  :35............................297
  :36............................297
  :39............................297
24:3............................154
  :5–9...........................154
  :12.............................28
  :14............................102
  :15.............................95

Leviticus (cont.)

24:16 2
  :23 12
25:36 246
26 250
  :2 78
  :11 250
  :31 78
  :34f. 119
27:29 2
  :30 . . . . **b**; 246
  :30ff. . . . . .246(2×)
  :32 246

Numbers

1:2 239
  :50 . . . . **55**; 236
  :50*b* 245
  :51 . . . . **1, 10, 42**; 6, 7
  :53 . . . . . **3, 5, 15, 17**; 45, 62, 75, 77, 260, 271
  :53*b* 245
3 . . . . **5, 55, 58, 61**
3–8 271
  :1 27
  :5–10 . . . . **5, 11**
  :6 . . . . **43**; 201
  :6*b* 245
  :6f. **5**
  :6–8 77
  :7 . . . . . . **5, 6, 11, 13, 48, 64**; 31, 33, 260(2×),
            262, 274
  :7*a*. **47, 48**, 245
  :7–10 3
  :8 . . . . . **5, 6, 11, 13, 64**; 27, 31, 260(3×), 262
  :8*a* 260
  :9 275
  :10 . . . . **1, 11, 46**; 6, 275
  :10*a* **23**; 80
  :11–13 . . . .**13**; 31
  :14–39 . . . .**58**; 235
  :15 239
  :23 233
  :25 . . . . .260, 263, 310
  :25f. **58, 64**; 233
  :28 . . . . .33, 51, 307
  :29 . . . . .197, 233
  :31 . . . . . **58, 64**; 51, 186, 233, 242, 260, 275,
            304, 310
  :32 . . . .**43**; 278, 306
  :36 . . . .**58, 64**; 233, 260, 263, 275, 310
  :38 . . . . .**1, 3, 5, 12, 45, 48, 55, 58**; 6, 31(2×),
            33, 41, 51, 78(2×), 79, 233
  :40 239
  :40–43 31
  :41 . . . .**13**
  :45 . . . .**13**

Numbers (cont.)

3:47 246
4 . . . .**5, 55, 56, 58, 59, 61**; 236, 271
  :1 239
  :1–20 . . . .**57**
  :2 . . . .**58**
  :3 227
  :3f. **67**
  :4 . . . .**57, 64**
  :4–15 . . . .**57**; 47
  :5–16 236
  :9 304
  :12 304
  :14 . . . . .219, 304
  :15 . . . . **2, 16, 33, 67**; 76, 186
  :15*b* **57**
  :15ff. **52**
  :15–20 . . . .**51**
  :16 . . . . **48**; 278
  :17f. **23**
  :17–20 236
  :18 216
  :19 . . . .**56, 64**
  :19f. **2, 33**
  :19*b* **60**
  :20 . . . .**16, 47, 48**; 128, 162
  :21 239
  :21–27*a* **57**
  :23 . . . .**58, 64**; 227
  :24 . . . .**56**(2×)
  :26 . . . .**65**; 275, 303
  :26*b* 316
  :27 . . . .**56**(2×), **58**
  :27*b* **57**
  :28 . . . . **48, 58**; 232, 278
  :30 . . . .**58**
  :30f. **64**; 231
  :31 . . . .**56**(2×), **57, 58**; 231
  :32 . . . .**57, 58, 65**; 231(2×)
  :32*a* 279
  :32*b* 51, 233
  :33 . . . . **48, 64**; 232, 278
  :35 . . . .**58, 64**
  :39 . . . .**58, 64**
  :43 . . . .**58,64**
  :47 . . . .**56**(2×), **58, 60, 64**
  :49 . . . .**56, 60, 64**
5:2 . . . . .157, 161, 166
  :5–8 88
  :6f. 86
  :25 141
  :25f. 141
  :31 95
6:7 . . . . .141, 257
  :19f. 102
  :20 86

Numbers (cont.)

7.....................................271
:5....................................**64**
:5–9..................................**57**
:7...................................230
:9............................**64**; 242, 257
:10*b*.................................141
:89...................................**43**
8.......................46, 110, 271(5×)
:5f...................................**28**
:7...................................278
:10...................................**28**
:11.......................**28, 61, 64**; 271
:12...................................**28**
:13...................................**28**
:14–19................................**13**
:15.......................**28, 61, 64**; 271
:16...................................275
:19.....**17, 27**(3×), **28, 29, 61, 64**; 110, 113,
        271, 272, 275
:19*b*................................98
:21...................................**28**
:22........................**61, 64**; 271(2×)
:23–26...............................271
:24...................................265
:24f..................................227
:24–26........................**5, 64**; 271(2×)
:25f.................................**54, 58**
:26..............................228, 245
9:6................................141(2×)
:13....................................95
:15ff..............................**43**; 170
:18–23................................37
:19.....................................6
:23.....................................6
10:21.............................78(2×)
12:5..................................170
15:30f................................**17**
:35..................................2; 9
16f................................**b, 13**
16–18.................................**14**
:9.....**13, 48, 61, 64**; 41, 69, 226(2×), 243
:9*b*..............................315, 317
:18f..................................**14**
:23ff.................................**51**
:32...................................**51**
:35...................................**13**
17:5.............................**14, 32**; 6
:11ff................................100
:11–15...................**13, 15, 29**; 75
:25...................................**51**
:27....................................75
:27–28................................**20**
:28......**2, 13, 15, 19**(2×), **29**; 26, 85, 277
18..........................**61**; 77, 110, 201
:1........**15, 20, 23**; 78(2×), 201, 216, 316

Numbers (cont.)

18:1*a*........................**20, 23**(2×)
:1*b*.......................**20, 23**; 275
:1–5..................................70
:1–6.................................216
:1–7.............**5, 13, 15, 20, 23**; 244
:1–24..........................**13, 19, 23**
:2......**23, 32**; 34, 201(2×), 211, 216, 275
:2*a*.............................**6**; 245
:2*b*.................................**38**
:2–4.................................**48**
:3.....**2, 5, 15**(3×), **20, 23, 29, 32, 33, 48,
        52**; 33(2×), 55, 76, 92, 99, 162, 186,
        211, 271, 274
:3*a*................**23, 29, 33, 47**; 245
:3*b*.....................**23, 47**; 236
:3–5.................................307
:3–7...................................**3**
:4.........**15, 32, 61**(2×), **64**; 6, 175, 271
:4*a*....................**73**(2×); 47, 211
:4*b*.................**58, 70, 82, 274**
:5......**17, 42**; 33, 47(2×), 70, 75, 82, 260
        316
:5*a*....................**24, 29**; 47, 79
:5*b*..............................**20**; 70
:6..................**61, 64**; 216, 271, 275(2×)
:7.....**1, 5, 13, 46**; 6, 7, 55, 57, 63, 76, 80,
        122, 229, 275(3×), 301, 302
:7*a*......................**23**(2×), **29**; 275
:8................................**68**, 246, 275
:8–20...............................275
:11..................................275
:12..............................246, 275
:19..............................246, 275
:21.....**b, 22**(2×), **61**(2×), **64**; 246(2×),
        271
:21*b*...............................**23**
:21ff................................246
:21–23......................**13, 20**; 275
:22.....**2, 11, 19, 20, 21, 23, 26, 29**; 26, 62,
        70, 85, 110, 277
:22f........................**13, 20, 27, 29**; 63
:23.....**15, 19, 20, 21, 23**(2×), **61**(2×), **64**;
        97, 271
:23*a*......................**20, 29**; 68
:23*b*...............................**22**
:24.......................**22**; 246(2×)
:26.................................246(3×)
:28.................................246(3×)
:29..................................246
:31................**23, 61**(2×), **64**; 246, 271
:31*b*...............................**23**
:32*a*................................98
19:9....................................**6**
:20....................................78
20:6..................................170

Numbers (cont.)

20:26–28	**48**
25:1–15	**46**
:4	**28**; 114, 119
:4a	**46**
:4b	**46**
:6b	**46**
:7b	**46**
:8b	**46**
:9	**46**; 75, 109
:9–13	119
:11	**28**
:12	114
:13	**28**, 46
:13b	110
:18f.	75, 109
26:1	239
27:1f.	141
:18	102
28	297
:18	297
:22	106
:25	297
:26	297
:30	106
29:1	297
:5	106
:7	297
:12	297
:35	295
30:16	**26**; 95
31:6	186
:16	75, 109
:19–24	186
:25–54	186
:30	**5, 58**; 246
:47	**5, 58**
:50	**28**; 108
:54	108
35:33	**28**
42:14	**32**
44:16	**33**

Deuteronomy

5:9	219
10:8	181, 186
11:1	**44**
:13, 16	301
12:2, 30	301
13:6	14, 214, 219
15:18	246
16:6	297
17:5	214
19:10	10
22:13f.	127
23:15	250

Deuteronomy (cont.)

24:16	222
31:9	186
32	251
33:9	181

Joshua

3f.	**62**
3:4	141
6:6	186
:12	186
7	118, 219
8:30ff.	**62**
9:27	41
17:4	141
18:1	**62**
22:3	**44**
:17	75, 109
:17f.	**28**
:20	75
:20b	119
:27	301

Judges

6:28	141
:31	212
9:24	10
19:13	133
20:13	10
:27f.	**62**
21:10f.	14, 219

1 Samuel

1–3	**62**(2×)
4:4	186
:17	75, 109
4–7	**62**, 186
6:4	75
:19	**16**; 21, 75
15:3b	14
:18	14
:9	286
16:22	201
17:20	29
:28	29
:54	48
21:5f.	127
:9f.	48
22:23	**44**
26:15f.	29
28:29	15

2 Samuel

6:6f.	**16**
7	247, 248(2×), 250
:6f.	**62**(2×); 250

2 Samuel (cont.)
```
8:7–11........................48
11:11........................62
15:24–29....................252
20:3.........................44
21:.....................118, 219
 :1.........................109
 :1–16.......................28
 :3.........................109
24..........................75
 :1ff........................28
 :21.........................75
 :25....................75, 109
```

1 Kings
```
1:2.........................201
 :38.........................41
2:5.........................44
 :7.........................126
 :26........................186
 :33.........................10
 :37.........................10
5:30........................292
6:5f........................47
 :10.........................47
7:14........................292
 :22........................292
 :40........................292
 :51....................48, 292
8:3–6.......................186
 :11........................169
 :64........................314
9:23........................292
10:5.........................48
 :17.........................48
11:28.......................292
14:26–28.....................48
 :28....................41, 48
20:39.......................208
 :42...................14, 208
21:10........................12
 :13f........................12
```

2 Kings
```
3:27........................114
10:24b.......................48
11:3a........................47
 :5..........................4
 :10.........................48
 :5ff........................29
 :5–9........................7
 :10....................48(2×)
 :18........................311
12:10..................178, 197
 :12........................293
 :15........................293
```

2 Kings (cont.)
```
12:16.......................293
14:6........................222
16:12.......................141
21:4.........................47
 :5..........................47
22:4...................47, 178
 :5........................293
 :7.........................47
 :8.........................47
 :9........................298
23:4..................178, 197
 :11.........................47
 :12.........................47
25:18.................178, 197
```

Isaiah
```
6:4.........................178
8:3.........................127
21:8.......................4; 44
 :11.........................29
22:11.......................295
28:21.......................295
32:6........................295
37:26.......................295
43:3........................114
53:4a........................97
 :5..........................97
 :11b........................97
 :12.........................97
54:14.......................133
66:1f.......................256
 :3.........................256
 :6.........................256
 :18b.......................256
 :20........................256
 :21........................256
 :23........................256
```

Jeremiah
```
3:17........................256
14:21.......................256
17:12.......................256
30–31.......................256
31:9.........................29
33:8–22.....................256
48:1........................295
50:25.......................295
52:24.......................197
```

Ezekiel
```
3:17ff.......................25
 :18.........................25
 :20.........................93
4:4.........................97
9:1.........................311
```

Ezekiel (cont.)

10:3f. 170
16:37. 127
18:4. 25
  :6. 127
  :13. 25
20:40. 319
22:26. ....**a**; 1
29:18. 246
33:1–9. 208
  :6. 25
  :8. 25
34:11f. 51
37:7. ....121(2×)
  :17. ....121(2×)
39:18. 243
40–42. 47
40–48. ....**73**
  :5. 47
  :39–42. ....**73**
  :44. 47
  :45. 47
  :45b. ....47(2×)
  :47. 47
  :48. 47
41:1. 47
  :4. 47
  :5. 47
  :5–11. 47
  :7. 47
  :8. 47
  :10. 47
  :11. 78
  :13. 47
  :14. 47
  :15. 47
  :17. 47
  :19. 47
  :20. 47
  :21. 47
  :23. 47
  :25. 47
  :26. 47
42:15. 47
43:27. 141
44:4. 47
  :5. ....47(2×)
  :6ff. 41, 47, 78
  :8. 40
  :8a. 41
  :8b. ....41(3×)
  :11. ....**6, 73**; 41, 47(2×), 226, 316
  :11a. 41
  :11b. 310
  :13. ....**33**
  :14. ....**73**(2×); 41(2×), 47(3×), 316

Ezekiel (cont.)

44:14b. 310
  :14ff. 41
  :14–16. ....**6**
  :15. 40
  :15a. 41
  :15f. **33**
  :16. 47
  :16b. 40, 41, 47
  :19. 58
  :20. 145
  :23. ....**a**; 1
  :25. 19
  :27. 149
45:4. ....78, 313
  :5. 313
  :18–20. 78
  :19. 211
46:1. 78
  :3. 78
  :6–8. ....**73**
  :9. 78
  :15a. 78
  :16a. 78
  :24. ....**73**; 78
48:11. ....**406**;

Amos

9:1. 179

Hosea

5:4. 257
12:13. 29

Joel

2:17. 166

Jonah

1:8. 295

Habakkuk

2:1. ....4; 44

Zephaniah

1:8f. 41

Haggai

1:14. 293

Zechariah

3:7. ....40, 44, 315

Malachi

1:7ff. 40
2:2. 40
  :11f. 40
3:5–9. 40
  :14. ....40, 44

Psalms

26:6. 211
43:3. 251
63:3. 149
78:28. 251
 :59f. 251
84:3. 251
91:10. 133
106:29. .75, 109
 :29f. **28**
107:23. 295
121:3ff. 29
132:. 257
 :5. 251
 :7. 251

Job

1:18. 212
10:17*b*. 276
14:14*b*. 276
18:21. 251
39:6. 251

Proverbs

11:8. 114
16:14. 114
21:18. 114
24:27. 286

Lamentations

1:8. 127

Esther

1:14. 125
3:9. 295
9:3. 295

Daniel

8:27. 295

Ezra

3:8. . . . . .227, 293
 :9. 293
8:20. 318
10:13. 295

Nehemiah

4:3. . . . . .44, 50
 :5. 294
 :9. 294
 :10. 294
 :11. 294
 :13. 294
 :15. 294
 :16. .44, 50, 294
5:16. 294

Nehemiah (cont.)

6:3. 294
 :9. 294
 :11. 22
 :16. 294
7:3. . . . . .44, 50, 212
10:33. . . . .**74**
12:25. 44
 :9. 44
 :45. . . . . .40, 44, 50
13:14. 44
 :30. 44

1 Chronicles

4:3. 50
 :16. 50
6:7. 306
 :33. 275
 :34. 141
7:3. 50
8:11. 48
9:13. . . . .**72**; 306
 :19. . . . .**72**; 178, 197
 :19*b*. 197
 :20. 184
 :22. 178
 :23. 44
 :26–32. . . . .**72**
 :26*b*. 177
 :27. . . . .**7**; 50
12:29. . . . .**4, 7**
 :45. 50
16:39. 258
17:5. . . . .**62**
21:14. . . . . .75, 109
 :22. . . . . .75, 109
 :26. 258
 :29. 258
 :30. 258
22:1. 258
 :15. . . . . .292(2 ×)
23:4. 292
 :24. . . . . .227, 305
 :25f. **63**
 :26. . . . .**72**; 257
 :26–32. . . . .**72**
 :27. 227
 :27–32. 258
 :28. . . . . .257, 307
 :28–32. 306
 :28ff. 307
 :29. 307
 :32. . . . . .44, 307
24:3. 306
25:6. . . . . .306, 309
26:12. 44

1 Chronicles (cont.)
26:16 141
27:24 . . . . .75, 109
  :26 295
28:10 78
  :13 204
  :13–15 72
  :20 305
  :20f. 292
29:1, 5 292

2 Chronicles
  1:3–6 258
  4:11 292
  5:1 292
  7:2 170
   :3 . . . . .43; 170
   :6 44
  8:14 . . . . .44, 306
   :16 292
 13:11 44
 17:7–9 308
   :13 286
 23:4 178
   :4–8 7
   :6 . . . . .44, 257
   :6–7 7
   :6ff. 47
   :9 48
   :13 234
 24:4–14 74

2 Chronicles (cont.)
 24:5f. 309
   :12 305
   :13 293
   :14 304
 25:1 306
 26:16 47
 29:16 47
   :25 47
   :34 226
 30:17 . . . . .73; 226
   :35 306
 31:2 306
   :16 . . . . .44, 306
   :17 227
   :21 306
 34:9 . . . . .47, 178, 197
   :10 293
   :12 293
   :13 . . . . .293, 305, 309
   :15 47
   :17 293
 35:2 . . . . .44, 306
   :3 . . . . .63; 257(2 ×), 306
   :6 . . . . .73; 257
   :10 306
   :11 . . . . .73; 226, 257
   :12 257
   :15 257
   :16 306

HELLENISTIC SOURCES

Philo

Moses, II, 174 53
On Rewards and Punishments, 74 53

Josephus

Antiquities
ix, 8:2 319
xiii, 3:5 161
Wars
v, 5:6–7 161

RABBINIC SOURCES

Mishna

Sheḳalim
. 321
Yoma
2:1 161
Sukka
4:5 211
Beẓa
5:2 297
Megilla
1:5 297

Mishna (cont.)

Baba Mezi'a
7:8 29
Sanhedrin
2:1 115
9:6 . . . . .7, 55
Zebaḥim
5:3 165
Bekorot
7:1 156

MISHNA (cont.)

Tamid
1:1f. 34
Middot
1:1, 6, 9. 34
2:6. . . . . .161, 211
4:6. 47
Kelim
1:8. 61
:9. . . . . .156, 157, 227,
Nega'im
1:12. 115
Para
3:11. 43
ch. 9. 43

TOSEFTA

Yoma
1:12. 161
Sukka
4:23. 166
Baba Ḳamma
7:6. 115
Sanhedrin
4:1. 115
Shebuot
1:4. 115
Kelim, Baba Kamma
1:6. 166
:11. 115
Para
3:14. 43
4:1. 115

BABLI

Shabbat
24b. 297
'Erubin
105a. 5
Pesaḥim
96a. 42
47a. 297
83b. 297
Yoma
1:12. 115
Megilla
13b. 27
Baba Ḳamma
40a. 115

BABLI (cont.)

Sanhedrin
83f. 199
83a. 7, 156
83b. 55, 148

YERUSHALMI

Sheḳalim
4b. 319
Sanhedrin
48b. 7

TANNAITIC MIDRASHIM

Mekilta of R. Simeon. 42
Sifra
Vayiḳra nedaba
par. 4:9f. 165
Zav
par. 2:12, 3:5. . . . . .34, 162
Shemini
par. 1:4. .144, 147
Aharei
13:15. 127
Emor
3:11. 143
par. 3:5. 156
Sifre Numbers
116. . . . . .7, 34, 55
124. 43
Sifre Zuta
Num. 5:2. . . . . .61, 156, 157, 161, 165
8:26. 228
18:2. 34
:3. . . . . .55, 162
:4. 175
:7. . . . . .7, 55
Beraita diMelechet haMishkan. 27

LATER MIDRASHIM

Leviticus Rabba
20:9. 148
Numbers Rabba
19. 234
Tanḥuma
Aharei 6. 148
Yalqut Shimoni
752. 175

ANCIENT NEAR EASTERN TEXTS

Egyptian
"Curses and Threats". 176
"The God and His Unknown
    Name of Power". 176

Egyptian (cont.)
"Repulsing of the Dragon". 176
Temple Inscriptions. 134

Hittite

"Daily Prayer of the King"..........132, 206

"Evocatio"............................176

"Instructions for Palace Personnel to
Insure the King's Purity".............217

"Instructions for Temple
Officials"...................**43, 46**; 189ff.

"Proclamation of Telepinus"............217

"Ritual for Purification of
God and Man".....................176

Mesopotamian

"Enuma Elish".......................176

Lipšur Litanies.......................133

Namburbi Texts......................133

New Year's Ritual....................176

Temple Kettle Drum...................176

Greek

Temple Inscriptions...................135